Doug BUFFONE

MONSTER · OF THE · MIDWAY

Doug BUFFONE

MONSTER · OF THE · MIDWAY

MY 50 YEARS WITH THE CHICAGO BEARS

as told to Chet Coppock

TRIUMPH BOOKS

Buffone, Doug, 1944–2015
Doug Buffone : Monster of the Midway : my 50 years with the Chicago Bears / Doug Buffone, as told to Chet Coppock.
pages cm
ISBN 978-1-62937-167-2
1. Buffone, Doug, 1944– 2015 2. Football players—Pennsylvania—Biography. 3. Chicago Bears (Football team)—History. I. Coppock, Chet, 1948– II. Title.
GV939.B82A3 2015
796.332092—dc23
[B]
2015012570

This book is available in quantity at special discounts for your group or organization. For further information, contact:

Triumph Books LLC
814 North Franklin Street
Chicago, Illinois 60610
(312) 337-0747
www.triumphbooks.com

Printed in U.S.A.
ISBN: 978-1-62937-167-2
Design by Patricia Frey

Photos courtesy of the author except where otherwise noted.
Title page photo courtesy of AP Images/Vernon Biever
Photo on page xix courtesy of Getty Images/Richard Stagg

To my wife and soul mate, Dana—just as beautiful now as you were the first day I met you.

Your love, warmth, and vitality brought new meaning to a guy who was dealing with life without shoulder pads and crowd noise. You gave me a giant spark of energy and a new sense of passion right from the get-go. You truly make me feel eternally blessed and eternally grateful.

My checks said I played for the Chicago Bears, but that's not really the whole story. The simple fact is, I played for the fans of Chicago, fans I love as much, or more, today than I did five decades ago.

—Doug Buffone
February 2015

Contents

Author's Note

Doug Buffone just wasn't supposed to leave us...at least not so soon. There were still too many belly laughs to be enjoyed, too many complaints to bring forth about the Bears offense, and too many days and nights of his brilliant football career to hash and then, for gosh sakes, rehash.

Sadly, I don't make the rules. None of us do.

Did I mention Doug's ever-present cigar that was never lit, but was chewed so badly it looked like a dead rat on a dirt road?

Monday, April 20, 2015, in Chicago dawned with an overcast sky and light rain. The day, in and of itself, seemed particularly somber. I was undergoing a physical exam at Rush when my phone became an explosion of texts and phone calls. I tried to be the "good" patient, but I finally gave in to the bell when I saw my son Tyler was on the line.

The kid didn't mince words. "Tip" simply told me, "Dad, Doug Buffone has passed."

It's strange how one reacts to the loss of a family member or a close friend. No matter how many times we see a loved one enter the landscape of death, somehow it always seems unfamiliar.

Frankly, my initial reaction to Buff's passing was that if the Bears know what's right they'll have their players wear a "55" patch in 2015 to honor this living, breathing success story who gave the club so many Sundays of ferocity.

Twitter and Facebook erupted with praise for Doug. You almost got the sense that people who had never seen him play but knew him by name or via his on-air work felt like they knew this hunk of leather from the Pennsylvania mining region. Is there such a thing as Twitter-bonding?

Forget about the legendary Will Rogers. Doug Buffone never met a man, woman, or child he didn't like. His gracious smile and the glowing warmth of his personality could do the impossible: melt Rahm Emanuel.

Bruce Rauner ran for governor on unlimited money. Doug should have sought the same position running on kindness. Number 55, we need one more lunch at Carmichael's or another argument about Jay Cutler over egg whites at the East Bank Club.

Dare I dream about the young kid out of Louisville who occupied the "Sam," the strong-side linebacker spot, for so many years in a Bears uniform? Why not? A young Doug Buffone—NFL player, saloon keeper, and Rush Street golden boy—was cool.

You know, Buff, you could have forced your way out of the Halas kingdom in the late '60s or early '70s by playing the role of bad actor. However, that wasn't you. Your passion for Chicago was unequaled. Gil Brandt and the all-powerful Dallas Cowboys were crazy in love with you.

They wanted you to play middle linebacker for Tom Landry. Yet, you never chose to leave. You wanted to play for those Bears fans who yearned to see you beneath the glowing lights of the postseason. I spent the night of your passing going back and forth with thought after thought about what was—and what might have been.

Doug, I guarantee you Larry Wolfe, your right-hand man and celebrated financial savant, and of course your wife, Dana, and a guy named Coppock will make your book happen.

We owe that to you.

I was blessed to spend considerable time with D.B. during his last year on this Earth. Time for which I shall forever be grateful. Hopefully, we constructed a read that will open eyes to a spectacular individual career that, all too frequently, was back-stopped by a bunch of clowns in Orange and Blue who would have been better occupied working as all-night managers at a 7-Eleven in Peoria.

Doug, it breaks my heart when I think about how enthused you were about the book tour we were planning. We already had numerous commitments. Time and again I thought about the yarns we'd spin on the road or how much we'd argue about the merits of new Bears heavyweights Ryan Pace and John Fox.

Just once I wish people could have heard you mutter, "I wonder if people care enough to read about me." Jeez Buff, for heaven's sake, you were larger than life. Your death put TV, radio, and the print media into overdrive.

I'll always remember WBBM-TV reporter Dana Kozlov coming by my West Loop residence to get my thoughts about you, a man I first met when Nixon was in the White House. I think a great deal of Dana Kozlov. She's a superb journalist, but how do you explain in a 35-second sound bite the reverence Dick Butkus had for you or the appreciation your Green Bay rival, Paul Hornung, had for your style of play? Yeah, the same Hornung you once leveled so badly that he had to leave a ballgame back in the '60s.

Of course, I cried. It broke my heart to see Dana and your twin daughters so horribly distraught. But I know Dana will never let the ship capsize. This gorgeous lady with a such a great sense of self and a remarkably loving soul couldn't live with herself if she let you down.

Doug, thanks for 45 years, pal, and especially for one magical year that truly reawakened my spirit.

Now, go argue contract money with George Halas. You just know the Old Man will relish the opportunity to square off against a bruising, yet intelligent, athlete who was everything the beloved Old Man sought in a Chicago Bear.

I love you, Doug. Of greater importance, Chicago, your town, will always love you...and truly never forget you.

—Chet Coppock
April 21, 2015

Foreword

I still feel honored that back in '79 a photographer took a picture of myself with Doug Buffone for the book *Halas by Halas.* I'll always treasure that.

I was very lucky. Early in my career, Doug, O.B., and Butkus took a liking to me. We used to have dinner together all the time at Morton's. You know, Doug was kind of like your cool cousin. When I first met him, he had restaurants and he also had his own magazine, *The Doug Buffone Chicago Bears Report.*

A lot of guys wanted to be just like him. I would just sit there and listen to them talk about how the game was supposed to be played. I'd say to Steve McMichael and Mike Hartenstein, "This is how we gotta play!"

Doug was unequivocally an inspiration to me.

Buffone didn't know it, but along with Dick and O.B., they gave me the hidden hymn of what the Bears preached as Monsters of the Midway.

Those guys were just great to me.

I like to think they saw some of themselves in me.

In '79, when I joined the Bears, I was green as grass. I'd been to one pro football game in my life. I really didn't know who Walter Payton was. I'd heard of him, just like I had heard about Doug. But I really didn't know him either.

I was a deer in the headlights.

It was Buffone's last year and we went through a brutal training camp under coach Neill Armstrong. I had become part of a small clique with Doug Plank, Hart, Gary Fencik, and Tom Hicks. Doug really wasn't the grizzled football player he'd been 10 years earlier, but guys marveled at his work ethic. Jeez, he was in with our trainer, Fred Caito, all the time, but you never saw him complain or beg off.

Nobody ever suggested that Buffone was the old gray mare. Not if you wanted to walk off the practice field on your own. You began to understand why the veterans on the club had such enormous respect for the guy. He just busted his ass.

You know the DNA of a football player is always illustrated by how hard he works when it's tough, when the pain is killing him. The aches, strains, and sprains were relentless. And don't forget the humidity. My gosh, the trees up at Halas Hall in Lake Forest were so thick that you felt like they were planted there to keep air out.

How can you practice when you can't even breathe?

I began to look at Doug like a daddy. You know, "Daddy goes to work. Daddy makes a living and feeds his family."

Too many guys who play this game never leave any kind of a footprint. Believe me, in that final year when Doug was a part-time linebacker and special team's guy, he left a massive footprint.

He always left footprints. He left his on me.

You just know the good guys. You can just smell 'em; I was lucky that Doug gave me a chance. I became the player I was because of him.

I love Doug Buffone.

Tell Coach Halas he can begin the new season. His linebacker is joining him.

—Dan Hampton

Preface

He deserved accolades, period.

Doug Buffone earned, but never received, Pro Bowl selections and those glamorous trips to Honolulu for the so-called NFL all-star game.

I have no memories of Howard Cosell or the zany Don Meredith raving about his talent and his distinct level of linebacking pride back in the 1970s when *Monday Night Football* was in its infancy.

Perhaps Doug Buffone was meant to play in a different era.

The kid from Louisville, by way of the Pennsylvania mining region, should have worn the Blue and Orange of George Stanley Halas and the Chicago Bears, back in the days when roughnecks like Joe Stydahar and Danny Fortmann, Pro Football Hall of Famers, led the legitimate "Monsters of the Midway," a team of beasts that won four championships from 1940 to 1946.

Those Bears savaged the rest of the league. For six years, they were the icing on the cake. The rest of the team scrambled for the crumbs. Throw in one of the greatest quarterbacks in NFL history in Sid Luckman, and the offense was as overpowering as the defense.

By contrast, the Buffone-era Bears thought it was a great Sunday if the offense scored 10 points by halftime.

You want to cry foul when you think about the 14 years Doug played for the Bears. There just weren't enough locker-room celebrations.

There were far too many Januarys spent thinking about football seasons that had been lost in the previous September. Doug was on the field for too many damn snaps that meant nothing.

The young Buffone had arrived in Chicago with big dreams.

He'd emerged from Louisville as a college All-American. He'd been honored as the Defensive MVP in the North-South game.

No less an authority than Weeb Ewbank quickly hopped on the Buffone bandwagon, telling Doug, that yes, he was a special guy with real talent. To hell with those kids from Notre Dame, Southern California, Ohio State, and other elite football factories. Weeb looked at Doug and saw a grinder, a nails-tough kid, who wouldn't back down if he was confronted by a mountain lion.

Doug Buffone was a *football* phenom in the basketball crazy state of Bluegrass mania.

Yes, Weeb Ewbank noticed.

He had coached Buffone's South team and loved the kid who played his guts out. Let's put it this way, Doug's passion for contact was so immense that he would race to grab his helmet to play on the kick return team.

Ewbank had already coached a pair of glamorous Baltimore Colts teams to world titles in 1958 and '59, led by the incomparable Johnny Unitas, along with guys like Lenny Moore, Gino Marchetti, and the beloved "Fatso" Artie Donovan.

Ewbank would later guide Joe Willie Namath and the New York Jets to Super Bowl glory over his old team, the Colts, on January 12, 1969.

A coach who knew what great players were all about and had won three NFL championships with them—he raved about No. 55.

The kid was special.

But championships were not in the cards for Buff. Not then, not ever.

Doug Buffone played on a 1–13 Bears team in 1969 that was actually one helluva lot better than the 3–11 club he suffered with four years later. It was like being asked to head up the defense for a fortification on the plains outside of San Antonio called the Alamo.

Buffone couldn't catch a break. His destiny was to play his heart out for a franchise muddling through mediocrity. Yet, to this day, Buff's heart and soul belong to the Bears. Sure, he will criticize the team when he believes it's fumbled, as he does in these pages, but in his heart Doug's love for the NFL's most storied franchise can never be questioned. Not by a soul. Never.

Was Doug to blame that he joined the Bears in '66 when the team *already* boasted Dick Butkus, perhaps the greatest single defensive player in pro football history?

The Butkus shadow was at once huge and, to a degree, unforgiving. It had no room for passengers. If Doug had 17 solo tackles versus Green Bay, the show, the spotlight always seemed to belong to "Crunch" Butkus.

Sayers and Butkus, the greatest one-two punch in draft-day history, chosen in Round 1 of the 1965 selection process. George Allen, a cerebral Halas sidekick, engineered this remarkable coup.

Butkus—the mere mention of his name, serves as an invitation to busted ribs, and there just weren't enough headline writers to accommodate the machine-like Buffone. Doug knew it and accepted it without rancor.

He played with guts and not for glory.

That's a pro, folks.

As Gale and Dick both limped their way out of the NFL in the early '70s, the woebegone Bears somehow became Abe Gibron's team.

If Doug had been hoping for a positive change leading to future team greatness, Big Abe was like a thunderstorm descending on a lit candle.

Greatness? Forget about it.

Gibron, a circus act in many respects, won the hearts of the local press for outrageous quotes and his unpredictable sideline demeanor.

But a winning team?

Abe was not an abbreviation for "able." He was a coach that defined exclamation points, not excellence.

Gibron is remembered by many older fans for the silly commercials he did for the Ford Motor Company with a local babe named Melody Rogers. While Abe fiddled, the Bears burned. The Monsters became mediocrity, a perennial NFL bottom feeder.

All the while, Doug Buffone suffered, losing in silence. In his own way, he suffered with class.

Did it ever get to him?

Passionate men hate losing. Doug oozed passion from every bone in his body.

Italian, you know.

God, losing sucks year in and year out. Of course, he felt the endless misery.

I do recall Doug popped off once on a TV program I was hosting on Channel 44, 40-plus years ago. The display of anger took place in late December 1971, when the Bears had somehow turned a promising 5–2 start into a 6–8 finish that had English professors searching for new words to describe the phrase "free fall."

Very simply, Buffone told me on live television, "I'm sick of losing. I'm sick of this crap."

Doug then went on to play *eight* more seasons with the Bears.

He spoke from his heart and then he went out and gave everything he had.

That's Doug Buffone. A man's man and the fan's man.

His star never rivaled the glamour linebackers—Butkus, Sam Huff, or Ray Nitschke—but when Bears' fans looked at Doug, they saw a winner, a kid who was a rock-solid chunk of consistency year in and year out.

He was beloved by everyone who watched him play because he never cheated his team, his character, or the fans who pledged allegiance to the Bears.

Football fans in Chicago are a cut above those in Jacksonville, Detroit, or, for heaven's sake, Arizona. They know when a guy is earning his checks and then some. They also know when a guy just doesn't have the winner's genes. See Cade McNown or Jay Cutler.

The losses kept piling up.

They left Doug in a state of anguish, which he remarkably kept in check. Over 186 games in a Bears uniform, he went out on that field every week and fought like a man possessed to somehow turn the inevitable tide of defeat into a win.

That's how things were done in his hometown of Yatesboro, Pennsylvania. It was the only way Buff knew how to play. He was the son of a coal miner and a cop. Go ahead, you do the math on that one.

To the regulars at Bears home games, he was a glistening ray of sunshine on an overcast football climate. They knew, despite epic losses, that Buffone was nothing if not a winner. The fans who knew football kept their eyes on the gladiators, the men who fought to the death on every play.

Yes, the kid with the dark complexion and the pronounced cheekbones (many people thought a young Buffone was Native American) who joined the Bears 50 years ago was always looked upon with pride. No. 55 symbolized another number...

One hundred ten percent.

In turn, Doug's remarkable charm and his genuine love for people and his city made him an iconic Chicagoan of the first magnitude.

I love Doug Buffone.

I respect and admire truly hundreds of athletes.

But, I *love* No. 55.

He always played at the highest level. He was everything Papa Bear George Halas wanted a Chicago Bear to be: tough, relentless, unselfish, and never-say-die. The old man loved guys who were glorified street fighters.

The wins and losses of an athlete don't always tell the true story.

Doug was more than a just another guy on the gridiron; he honored the game. If you'd lined him up behind Mean Joe Greene, Ernie Holmes, and L.C. Greenwood in Pittsburgh, Buffone would have been a Pro Bowl regular.

He would have been a Pro Bowl fixture.

And a Hall of Famer.

In my book, he was all those things. He was worthy of all those honors whether official or not. This was a great football player and more importantly, this was a great man.

Pal, this is your book.

In your words.

It is my hope that the world will see you for who you were, on and off the field.

My deepest thanks to you for allowing me to be a part of your printed legacy.

It has been a pleasure.

—Chet Coppock

chapter 1

Yatesboro...Raised in a Mining Town

You load 16 tons what do you get?
Another day older and deeper in debt.
St. Peter don't ya call me 'cause I can't go.
I owe my soul to the company store.
—Tennessee Ernie Ford "Sixteen Tons"

CHET COPPOCK: Were so many people that naïve?

When Ford released his chartbuster in 1955, some people saw it as a happy-go-lucky tune about life in the mills. In reality, Ford, blessed with a magnificently rich baritone, was shedding musical tears for the plight of those people who seemed, at birth, to be glued forever to the physical and mental anguish of life in the mines.

Nothing else, just the mines and family and, maybe, religion.

Samuel Fred Buffone, Doug's father, could relate to Ernie Ford's mournful lyrics. No one had to tell him about black lung or the ever-present danger of working in a coal mine.

Sam began working the mines when he was in the sixth grade.

The job carried a big slice of heartbreak. Samuel lost a brother one day when the mine collapsed on him. The company paid for his brother's funeral.

Always the company and yes, Sam Buffone and his family always shopped at the aforementioned company store.

Damn near everybody in Yatesboro, Pennsylvania, struggled through life toting their lunch pails to and from the mine. It was the only existence most of the local folks really knew.

You were born. You worked the mine. And you died.

That's just the way it was.

Sam Buffone was lucky.

And smart.

After 30-plus years of grime, unbearable heat, and bone-jarring cold, along with aches that never took a day off, he got a job as a local cop.

However, he had trouble adjusting to his new career.

Doug will tell you that his father's rough-edged approach to life didn't really make him a fit for police blue. Samuel had his own kind of discipline.

With Sam, it wasn't necessarily, "We serve and protect." It was more like, "Don't screw around with me."

This was a very intense guy who was looking to imbue his hard-nosed way of life into his children.

Enter Douglas John Buffone.

DOUG BUFFONE: I don't think my dad ever made more than $6,000 a year. He was a tough man. He had forearms like Popeye and a voice like Dean Martin.

We did all our shopping at the company store and we lived in a company home. Our whole life revolved around the company. Damn near everybody's did. Really, it was all we knew.

I didn't have an expensive meal at a first-class restaurant until I went to Louisville to play football.

Our house didn't have any indoor plumbing. I bought a new house... with plumbing, with my rookie signing bonus ($20,000) from the Bears.

Now, think about this. I was raised in the late '40s and early '50s and we had an outhouse. That's why I loved to play football, basketball, and baseball during high school. It meant I could actually take a shower every day.

It also meant that during the winters, I had to go out and shovel coal to keep the rest of the family warm. There were seven kids and we lived in a four-room house made up of two bedrooms, a kitchen, and a living room.

Baseball at Bluegrass in 1964. (I'm in the second row, third from the right.) I'll go to my grave convinced I could have played big league baseball. My cousin Jerry (second row, far right) just oozed talent.

That's it.

Once a month, sewage guys would come along with a giant hose and retrieve the waste from the outhouse into a truck. They were called honey dippers. It was really country. I guess maybe 500 people lived in our town.

The area was a melting pot. We had Italians, Germans, Poles, and Irish. We were all poor. We used to call wealthy guys "cake eaters," families that were so rich that they "could have their cake and eat it, too."

We didn't hate them, but we sure as hell resented them.

I can remember when I was real young, I wandered over to a cake eater's house and this old man screamed at me, "Get off my lawn, you goddamn Dago."

Jeez, I didn't know what the word meant. So, I went home and asked my Pop, "What's a Dago?"

I really can't remember what dad said to me, but I'll never forget this. The old man went over to the guy who called me a Dago and just beat the living shit out of him.

Dad used to work out on a speed bag. The cake eater never knew what hit him.

Dad was a really nice guy, but everyone knew: "Don't piss him off."

I'm third from the right on our high school football team—of course, I played both ways. (Also, my cousin Jerry, second from the left, and my best pal John Kulick, far right, were on the team.)

COPPOCK: You were a pretty good athlete, too.

BUFFONE: Yeah, I played the big three: football, basketball, and baseball.

COPPOCK: Long before Tommy Lasorda became the High Priest of all things "Dodger Blue," he began his career with "Dem Bums" as a scout.

This was back in the early '60s, long before Lasorda took over the Dodgers' lineup card from Walter "Smoky" Alston. And Lasorda has told me on a number of occasions that the best catcher he had ever scouted was Doug Buffone.

BUFFONE: I really loved baseball, even more than football.

I didn't like watching games, but I loved to play ball. There was something about hitting a home run that I just loved. So, I'm playing three sports and I'm also playing the trumpet.

Lasorda said to me, "I want you to be part of the Dodgers." Tommy sold me hard. Tom also wanted to sign Joe Namath, who was from Beaver Falls, about an hour away from Yatesboro.

He said he'd give me $6,000 if I signed. I'd never seen any money in my life. I really wanted to sign.

But my mother, Adeline, and my old man told me they wouldn't let me sign. They were determined that I was going to go to college. I was a good student in high school. They were right about college.

I had one other option.

I was serious about becoming a priest. I even met with our local padre to talk about my future. We were a very close town when it came to religion. I was thinking about it as a vocation.

However, when I told my dad I was thinking about becoming a priest, he looked me right in the eye and said, "What are you, a moron?"

Shortly after that, I lost my virginity in Yatesboro.

My old man knew that his kid was on testosterone overload.

chapter 2

The Legend of Ruffi

COPPOCK: A profile of young Doug with the tough dad is emerging. Tell us the story of the dog that flew south because you guessed wrong.

BUFFONE: Ruffi, the Wonder Beagle.

COPPOCK: Your dog growing up.

BUFFONE: Actually, my old man's dog. They always went hunting together.

COPPOCK: I can almost see Sam Buffone, after a long day in the mines, drenched in sweat and grime, coming home to his wife and seven kids and finding a large degree of solace and comfort with his beloved beagle curled up next to his ankles.

BUFFONE: It always seemed like Dad worked at least 10 hours a day. He wasn't going to walk away from overtime. If there was a chance to make a few extra dollars, he was gonna grab it.

COPPOCK: I have this vision of Sam closing his eyes and heaving a huge sigh of relief as he tenderly pet Ruffi, while his kids argued over watching *The Beverly Hillbillies* or *The Fugitive.*

Perhaps, he looked over at his beleaguered wife and wondered just how in the hell she kept the clothes moving from generation to generation, patching holes and darning socks to get just one more season out of a pair of hand-me-down, dime-store Argyles.

BUFFONE: (Smiling) I admired the work ethic of my old man and a mother who just wasn't allowed to get sick, making sure we always had clothes. They helped shape my never-ending persistence on the football field and in life. I knew at an early age I wanted out of Yatesboro. I determined early on that I wasn't going to look back.

Every night, when my dad got home, he looked forward to being with his buddy, Ruffi. That little beagle was a highlight of his life, a comfort at the end of the day.

COPPOCK: Yeah, we're here to celebrate the legacy of good old Ruffi. The fact is that the old timers will tell you they just don't make 'em like "the Ruffster" anymore.

BUFFONE: Poor Ruffi.

My dad and his dog. You have to understand a few things before we really settle into this story.

From the time I was in the second grade, I was around guns. I never feared them because they were just an accepted part of our lives.

If you went through our house, we had 12, 16, and 20-gauge shotguns as well as handguns. I think the first time I ever shot a rifle was when I was seven years old. Remember this, besides working the mines, my dad was also a cop.

COPPOCK: With just four rooms and all that artillery, did you ever run out of space to sleep?

BUFFONE: We damn near did. Dad really loved to go out and hunt. I know it took his mind off the drudgery of his job, but you have to understand the bigger picture.

From the time I was six years old, I knew that if my old man bagged a deer, that "trophy" wasn't going to find its way to our living room wall. It sure as hell wasn't going to be mounted.

My dad, Sam, and my brother Sammy transcend sports. They are true heroes.

It was going to find its way to a frying pan.

Hell, Bambi wouldn't have lasted.

Dad treated hunting as a part-time job. I guess he saw the so-called "sport" of what he was doing, but it was really about putting groceries on the table. Wealthy people, dentists, doctors, and lawyers would come in from the Pittsburgh suburbs to hunt. To them, it was just a game.

To us, it was dinner.

COPPOCK: And Ruffi was Sam Buffone's point man, so to speak.

BUFFONE: I was about 14 years old and was with my dad and his dog as we hunted deer, raccoons, squirrels, rabbits, and maybe even an occasional bear.

One day, I was carrying a 12-gauge when I saw a white-on-white rabbit. Ruffi was trying to outrace him. Well, I fired my rifle and I really thought I had bagged the sucker.

After my shot, my dad yelled out, "Did you get him?"

I was squinting into the brush and said, "Dad, I'm not sure." I looked again and then I blurted out, "Dad, I think I shot Ruffi."

Well, my father races over and there's his poor dog lying on his back with his paws up in the air.

Straight up.

You can't make this shit up. Poor Ruffi was history, paws up, dead as a door nail. I hate like hell to say this, but it really was funny.

But my old man went nuts. He yelled at me: "You dumb son of a bitch, ya killed Ruffi."

COPPOCK: Did your dad call a priest?

BUFFONE: No, I wish he had called for the last rites. That would have been easier. Instead, the old man's eyes were blasting a hole right through me. He was groaning about Ruffi and told me to get my ass home and come back with a shovel.

He made me dig a grave for Ruffi.

I dug and dug until, finally, I'm maybe three feet into the ground, and I asked the old man if I could stop.

He just screamed at me, "Keep on digging." Hell, I began to think I was digging a hole for the dog and me.

Listen, my old man lived to be 94 years old. He didn't hang around that long because he was soft or easygoing. He was adamant that Ruffi was going to leave with class.

I really didn't understand this at the time, but when Ruffi went down, Dad was sad because he'd lost a dog he truly loved. But, there was more to it than that.

Dad knew he was probably never going to find another dog as good as Ruffi. A dog that helped him feed me and my six brothers and sisters. That little guy was his partner in bringing home the bacon.

COPPOCK: Did you tell your dad with any kind of a break you would have bagged the rabbit and not Rin Tin Tin?

BUFFONE: Of course. But the old man didn't want to hear my lame-ass excuse that Ruffi had jumped in at the last instant. All I really remember was him barking at me, "Keep on digging."

In my own way, I probably felt worse than my dad did. I loved hunting. It was very exciting to me. I guess it gave me a youthful sense of adventure. Nowadays, I have a tough time pulling the trigger if I see a deer prancing around.

COPPOCK: For the record, Senator Buffone, I feel the same. I've said for years that I'd be happy to declare hunting a sport if they gave some poor doe or fawn a rifle and let them shoot back.

BUFFONE: I get that, but here's what you have to understand. Hunting was so much a part of what Yatesboro and the surrounding small towns were all about. It was a way of life for us. Sure, guys would boast when they nailed a big deer, but for most of the families, it was almost like a business.

Guys were trying to feed hungry mouths.

Deer are beautiful animals, but the farmers were allowed to shoot all of them they wanted because the damn things would just chew the hell out of their corn crops. You have no idea how much damage one buck can do to a guy's field.

COPPOCK: That tells me the fine art of poaching had to be a necessity.

BUFFONE: Sure it was. On the first day of hunting season, the whole damn town wore "hunting red" outfits. In a way, you were competing as much against your next door neighbor as you were against the animals.

Speaking of which, I've got to tell you this story about how hunting cost me a year of high school basketball.

COPPOCK: Where the hell are you going? Since when did hunting and hoops share the same platform?

BUFFONE: You're going to love this, Coppock.

Every year, from the time I was a little kid, my dad took me out for the opening day of hunting season. We were out before 5:00 in the morning. I loved it.

Well, in my sophomore year at Shannock Valley High School, my old man, as usual, took me out on Day One of the hunting season. That pissed the living daylights out of a guy named Hoffman who was our head basketball coach.

Hoffman and I never hit it off. The guy was crazy. He wanted us all to be skinheads. He thought crew cuts were too long. Well, I told him that I wasn't going to cut my hair.

Hey, I was the best player he had on his basketball team. I averaged damn near 30 points a game. I poured in points before the term "pure shooter" became part of the basketball language.

COPPOCK: So who wins this great conflict?

BUFFONE: Hoffman.

He got the team together and said, "Mr. Buffone seems to think that he should coach this team, but there is only one coach and that coach is me."

The son of a bitch kicked me off the team.

COPPOCK: This has a vibe that reminds me of the movie *Hoosiers*, where the mythical Indiana town of Hickory, population of about 150 people, is up in arms over the town's new head basketball coach, Norman Dale, played brilliantly by Gene Hackman, who's about as beloved as a swarm of lepers.

Hackman kicks a couple of players off the team and they come back repentant. They added Jimmy Chitwood and the club went on to win the state title.

BUFFONE: (Laughs) My story didn't quite play out that way. This wasn't a Hollywood movie.

Hoffman really took his lumps. The school principal tried to talk him into letting me play. I thought my old man was gonna kill him. The whole town really rallied to my support. Everybody was up his ass trying to force him to play me.

He never bent.

Looking back now on what Hoffman did, I have to admire the guy. He never backed down. The team had a lousy year, but Hoffman had taught me a lesson: you can't have a separate set of rules, even for a superstar, on a young team. All your players have to follow the same path.

COPPOCK: I know for years you used to go hunting every fall to see your brothers and hang out with old pals.

BUFFONE: That was a Buffone tradition.

However, it really began to change for me in 2013. I shot a beautiful deer, and I have to be frank—the sight of the poor animal whining in helpless pain before it died just broke my heart.

Really, when I would go back to Yatesboro to hunt, it was all about camaraderie, catching up with guys you just don't get to see often enough. I used to sit up in a tree stand for 10 or 12 hours, waiting for my big opportunity. I also hunted with my brothers: Joey, Sammy, and Dennis.

Now, I just don't think I could take an animal out, not even a squirrel.

I also stopped hunting on the day the deer stand busted and part of the structure broke, and a piece of it damn near went up my ass. I wasn't thinking deer. I was thinking *proctologist.*

I was sitting with John Kulick, my best friend, when this happened. Naturally, he laughed like hell.

You know when I really think about the last 10 years, I didn't really give a damn about landing any big prizes. I know there were times when I shied away from pulling the trigger when I had a small deer in my range.

I just couldn't do it.

But I guess you're a product of your background, your growing-up years. If I was out with the guys right now and had the chance to land a big buck, I might go for it.

The average guy on the street doesn't know this, but hunters do. Deer are so damn smart. They're uncanny; they can smell our scent. They also know how to camouflage themselves.

I remember one year, one of those bastards hid under leaves about 100 feet away from me for about nine hours. I don't know how in the hell he did it. Finally, darkness began to settle in and I had absolutely no chance to nail him. I mean no chance at all.

COPPOCK: All these hunting tales remind me of one of my most cherished Doug Buffone stories.

You were booked to appear on one of my Bear Luncheon shows at Ditka's old restaurant on Ontario Street in '88, just after one of your hunting expeditions. I'd bet the rent that you had flown in from Pittsburgh on the Tuesday morning before our give and take with the audience.

I recalled that you hadn't seen the game from that Sunday or any of its highlights. Hell, you hadn't even looked at the box score. If memory serves me correctly, you did ask me one rather enlightening question: "Who won?"

However, the audience thought you were inside the huddle barking out signals along with Jim Harbaugh.

You were just great.

Every time I brought up Harbaugh, you talked Bobby Douglass. Every time I talked Singletary, you talked O.B. and Butkus.

It was really memorable theater.

I recommend this to any current Chicago Bear preparing for an off day, speaking engagement, or a luncheon banquet—go on a hunting trip.

Apparently, it opens your eyes in ways the human race just can never comprehend.

BUFFONE: Except when I shot Ruffi.

COPPOCK: Yeah, when you killed the pride and joy of Papa Sam.

chapter 3

Here Come the Hillbillies

COPPOCK: I don't want to shock anybody, but Doug Buffone's growing-up years in the tiny hamlet of Yatesboro, Pennsylvania, were not milk and cookies at bedtime.

No one was going to confuse Sam Buffone with Mr. Rogers.

Still, Doug oozes passion for a glowing mom who was always there for her children and a rough, no-nonsense father who was stoic as all hell on the outside, but had a soul that was drenched in insatiable kindness for his wife and kids.

BUFFONE: My old man was a tough son of a bitch. God, he was driven. He had to be.

Every day, he knew he had a family that completely relied on him. He came across as very indifferent, but those who knew him knew what he had endured all those years in the mines and knew he had a big heart.

COPPOCK: I have this vision of your dad fighting exhaustion, somehow surviving the life-draining job of a coal miner with hands that looked and felt like thick, black leather. He never complained and never felt sorry for himself.

He played the cards he was dealt. He found a way to endure because in reality, he had no alternative. He just had no choice. End of issue.

BUFFONE: You know my mom and dad hardly ever saw me play football, basketball, or baseball in high school. People ask me if that bothered me.

It really didn't.

I understand that my mom had to be in seven places at once and that my dad was always focused on how in the hell he was gonna get food on the table for me and all of my brothers and sisters.

That was more important to me than seeing him in the bleachers.

Dad's first love wasn't football or basketball. He loved boxing. He was like a relentless fighter in a 15-round title bout. He loved Rocky Marciano.

I think about all the time he spent in the dark confines of the mines, the endless hours, sweat pouring out of his body, the feeling of just getting by, making it to the next round and somehow always answering the bell.

I mean just getting by and never taking the eight count.

I grew up just like him.

I think the old man loved to lace on the gloves and punch anything, just to get rid of the pent-up frustration he had inside him. Dad always figured the best way to settle any dispute was with his hands.

He was a tough son of a bitch. Again, he had to be. He didn't like to see weakness.

You know most of my siblings still live in Yatesboro. The hero in my family, my brother Sam, left college to join the Marines to fight in the Vietnam War. Can you imagine how my mom felt when Sammy ditched his scholarship at Sam Houston State to enter the armed services?

Sammy had strong beliefs and he truly felt he should be defending the United States against Communism in Southeast Asia.

Jesus, I remember him sending us a photo with him holding a gun over his head and a note that read, "They'll never take me alive." My mother had to deal with that. It was torture. I don't know how she endured that. For Christ's sake, think about that. His commitment was so damn sincere he was ready to die for the United States.

For some of my family and my extended family, sports became a way out. I had brothers and cousins who all earned scholarships to colleges because they could either play football or hit a fastball 450 feet.

COPPOCK: Speaking of getting out of town, I have heard about you and your crazy car stories. Is it safe to say that your father never looked upon you as "King" Richard Petty?

BUFFONE: Please, don't get me started. I had a couple of, shall we say "situations" with my old man's car that just blew the lid off the damn roof. Christ, did I make the old man mad.

COPPOCK: The green flag drops, fire away Mario Andretti.

BUFFONE: You're gonna think this is nuts. But it's completely on the square. A couple of times I just beat the shit out of the old man's beloved cars. Do you remember the old Chryslers with those big fins on the back?

Well, one day, I'm pulling out of the garage and everything is fine. I get the car out and go back to shut down the garage door. Obviously at the time, we didn't have any automatic garage door openers.

Well, I made a slight error. When I got back in the car, I thought I had the sucker in reverse.

I guessed wrong.

I floored the damn car and I smacked right into our garage door.

COPPOCK: What did Sam say about your driving brilliance?

BUFFONE: I got out of the car and ran like hell. I was scared shitless. I thought the old man would tear me apart. I just kept running until he had time to cool off.

Dad had to look at that car and saw money he didn't have, wrapped in a battered car and a shattered garage door.

COPPOCK: Is that the main reason why you bought your parents a new house with the twenty large in bonus money you got when you signed with Halas?

BUFFONE: (Laughing) I had put them through so much shit. I bought them a new home just to honor them. It gave me a magnificent sense of pride.

It was my way of saying thanks to two people who absolutely loved each other. I mean, my dad would have laid down and died for my mom and she would have done the same thing for him.

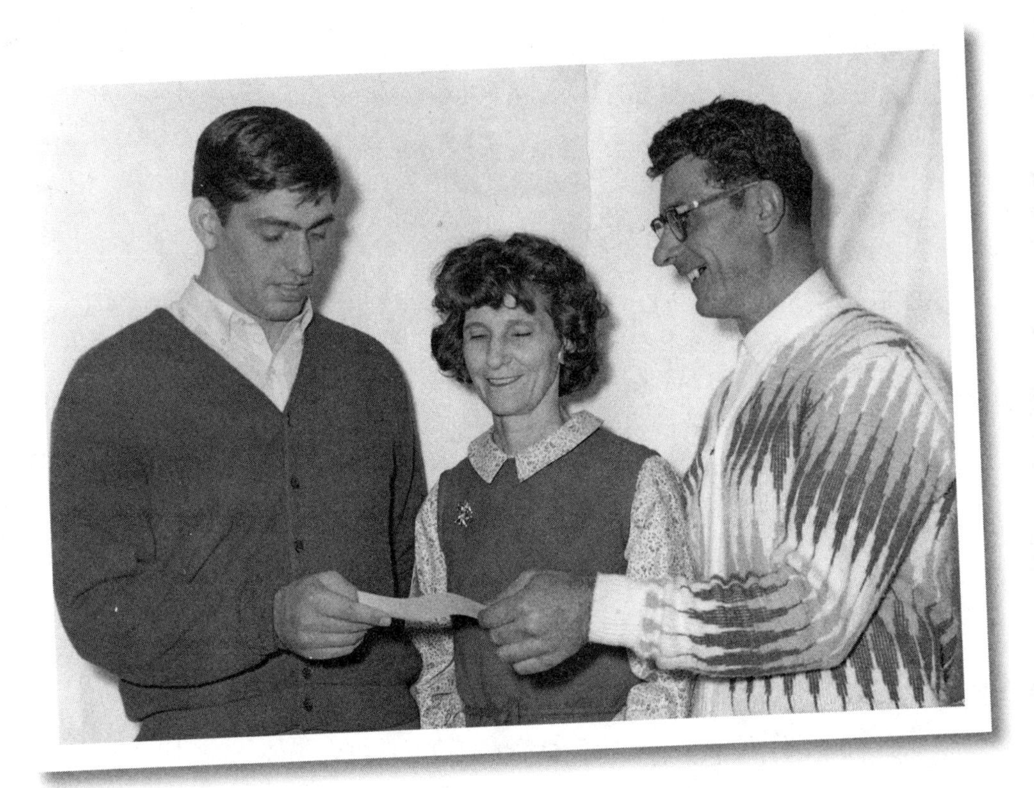

Perhaps my proudest moment: handing my signing bonus from George Halas to my mom and pop.

My mom was really ahead of her time. She's the greatest people person you could ever hope to meet. She really had a little P.T. Barnum in her personality. I have no doubt she would have been a public relations whiz if she'd ever found her way to Chicago or New York.

COPPOCK: Your mom was obviously a very unique lady. She even touched the Old Man. George Halas was clearly impressed by Adeline, and even his attitude toward you was rich with love and admiration.

The Papa Bear didn't toss out compliments every 15 seconds. He just wasn't built that way. But Ma Buffone got to him.

BUFFONE: My mom was really special. She was the valedictorian of her high school class.. It's a shame that she never had the chance to go to college. But, my mom earned a "Ph.D" in promoting a guy named Doug Buffone.

As proof, she personally phoned Howard Cosell at halftime of a *Monday Night Football* game we were playing and wanted to know why Howard wasn't giving me more buildup. To this day, I have no idea how her call got through to Cosell.

But, during the second half, Howard spoke several times about Mrs. Buffone and her affection for her son. I gotta figure at the time that it would have been easier to find Jimmy Hoffa than it was to reach Howard Cosell.

Think about that. What mom does that sort of thing and gets away with it?

COPPOCK: Your beloved parents—you had a special name for them.

BUFFONE: Mom and Dad didn't get to see many of my high school games, but they were regulars at my football games at Louisville. I nicknamed them "the Hillbillies" because they'd pack a bunch of people in one car and drive down to see me play.

All they were missing was Granny Clampett sitting on top of the car holding a shotgun. It was a sight to see.

Of course, just getting to the game was not enough. They were hillbillies; they had no shame. Mom would always be selling me left and right to Frank Camp, my coach at Louisville. I'd tell her she was embarrassing me. It didn't deter her in the least. It only made her more driven to tell everybody how special I was.

Sam was stoic. He really didn't say much because Mom said more than enough for both of them. Mom could turn out 190 words a minute.

Later when I joined the Bears, Mom became a gag line on our club. I recall when she arrived for one of our games, one of our guys said, "Look out, here she is!"

She was a rock star in a charming redneck kind of way. Guys really got a kick out of Adeline Buffone.

COPPOCK: Were they ever a distraction?

BUFFONE: Oh, hell yes.

I was on the road for a ballgame early in my career with the Bears, when the phone rang in my room at 4:30 in the morning. Being awakened like that wasn't good news because I always had trouble sleeping on game days.

It was the Hillbillies.

My old man was on the house phone in the lobby.

He said hello and told me that their party had no place to stay. So, now I'm on the spot. I called our trainer, Fred Caito, in his room. You can imagine how thrilled Freddie was to get a call at 4:30 AM.

I told him, "My family is down in the lobby—Jed, Granny, Jethro, all of them."

Freddie mumbled, "What in the hell are they doing down there?"

He was being too logical. He didn't quite grasp the Buffone way.

COPPOCK: Did you get the Hillbillies a room?

BUFFONE: Damn right I did.

Freddie came through, but I had to give my parents a message. I told them that they couldn't just show up unannounced in the middle of the night. I told them that they had to give me some kind of notice.

COPPOCK: Twenty bucks says they didn't understand?

BUFFONE: Of course not, no way, not a chance. You know Mom was just crazy about football. I mean, she really loved the game. My dad was really kind of detached about it. Mom would talk to anybody. She loved chatting with people.

She would always tell me, "Dikey, you have to sell yourself."

Dikey was my nickname. How about that one, huh?

COPPOCK: Dikey… what the hell is that supposed to mean? What did you do as a kid, bail out Holland?

BUFFONE: No, just Dikey.

COPPOCK: The whole picture becomes very lucid here. Your old man played the heavy. It was the only role he could play with you and your brothers and sisters. Yet, you knew he had your back.

On the other hand, your mom was this remarkable lady who raised seven kids but still had time to utilize this unique public relations gift. You should have had her sweet talk your high school basketball coach. You might have been Pennsylvania Player of the Year.

Your dad's toughness manifested itself in Doug Buffone, the football player, a guy who, even at the end of his career, played every goddamn down as a fourth-quarter goal-line stand in the Super Bowl.

The idea of going through the motions, playing soft, when you were down by four touchdowns, would have been an insult, a slap in the face to Sam Buffone.

BUFFONE: Yep.

COPPOCK: Conversely, your mom's relationship with you created a guy who felt perfectly normal opening the "Nickel Bag" when he was really still just a kid. A young guy in his early twenties in Chicago. Your mom provided you with the gift, with the wisdom to know how to sell and market the most precious commodity that a young Doug Buffone possessed... Doug Buffone.

But I still wanna know how your mom got to Cosell.

BUFFONE: Mom was just a PR bulldozer. She coulda been a linebacker.

COPPOCK: Now, I have a rough idea why you were.

chapter 4

Off to Blue Grass Country

COPPOCK: Can we assume you ran into your share of jealousy during your high school days in the tiny town of Yatesboro, P.A.?

I mean, really, let's examine the big picture.

You were all-everything as a football, basketball, and baseball player.

Plus, you eschewed "Introduction to a 9-Ball" and "The Illustrated History of Scrabble" to concentrate on legitimate college preparatory courses.

You excelled academically, gaining honor-roll status, while studying Algebra, Geometry, Chemistry, and French. Buffone? French? I guess Yatesboro had declared Latin a dead language.

In addition, your football jersey, No. 73, was eventually retired by Shannock Valley High School. That was a precursor towards you being inducted into the Pennsylvania Sports Hall of Fame.

But here's the $64 question. Why would a kid from the rolling hills of Western Pennsylvania decide to take French?

BUFFONE: That's a good question. I don't think I remember more than nine words of the damn language. I think "merci" is about as far as I go.

As for jealousy, I never felt a bit of it; not for a second. You see, I wasn't the first kid from our high school to be a so-called star athlete.

Chester, do you remember a guy named Bob Pellegrini?

COPPOCK: Damn right, the guy is on my all-time, all-underrated linebackers list along with you and Myron Pottios, the guy who played for the Steelers back in the '60s.

There were many things I could do at Louisville, but posting up future NBA MVP Wes Unseld wasn't on the list.

Pellegrini was one tough son of a bitch.

Bob was drafted out of Maryland by the Philadelphia Eagles in 1956, and later played on Buck Shaw's 1960 Eagles club that beat Vince Lombardi and the Packers at old Franklin Field in Philly to win an NFL title. It was the only title game loss Lombardi suffered during his magnificent tour as head coach at Green Bay.

But, here's what always knocked me out about Pellegrini.

I don't have to tell you that the Heisman Trophy is about guys like "Johnny Football" and "The Juice." It's a *skill position* award. Always has been.

In 1955, Bob was playing center and linebacker for Maryland. Offensive center for gosh sake. Somehow he commanded enough respect and attention to finish sixth in the Heisman race.

So, draw your own conclusion. Either Maryland had a PR machine that rivaled Lady Gaga or Anna Kournikova or Pellegrini was beyond a monster of a football player.

BUFFONE: He was our first Yatesboro star. Pellegrini never knew it, but he really was invaluable to me. Every young athlete really needs a hero to follow. I followed Bob.

You see, since we both went to the same high school, people were already conditioned to a big man on campus. So, really, I never felt that anybody was quietly hoping I would fail or blow out a knee. If anything, I always felt that people were rooting for me to get out of Yatesboro and make my mark elsewhere.

Just like Bob did.

COPPOCK: That tells me you never encountered the "small-town" mentality that a lot of guys face. You know what I'm talking about.

When I was a sportscaster in Indianapolis back in the '70s, I ran into some kids from very small towns near Indy who really felt that people scorned them because they wanted to get the hell out of Hicktown, U.S.A., and play in the big leagues.

BUFFONE: That's it in a nutshell.

Plus, I never tried to big time anybody. I just didn't think that was cool. I wasn't walking around town with the feeling that I was any better than anyone else just because I could play football.

I know with some people in Yatesboro there had to be a feeling of futility. People struggled. Most of them had tremendous pride, but the lives they lived were full of anguish and that just tore them apart. There were some people who eventually just looked at the place as a symbol of futility, misery. When you're a third-generation coal miner, you begin to ask yourself if hope actually exists.

When I got to college, I did have a small fear of failure.

I dreaded the idea of having to go back to Yatesboro and work in the mines. I only went into a mine once and that was enough. My old man took me down there one morning. We had to lie down on this roller that transported us about a mile into the mine. It was pitch black. It made me realize what my father had to go through to make a living.

It was hell.

He picked coal by hand. He wasn't paid by the hour, he was paid by the load. It was brutal work. I swore I'd never go in that mine again.

And I never did. The mines were always a built in fear factor that motivated me. It broke my heart when I saw—firsthand—what my pop had to endure. No human being should have to endure that kind of life. It was hell on earth.

COPPOCK: When you look back on your college football career, do you sometimes wonder how you were able to avoid landing at legendary Indiana University...the school in the thriving metropolis of Indiana, Pennsylvania? Side note: Indiana University of Pennsylvania tried to recruit Norm Van Lier to play football.

BUFFONE: (Laughing) It's not the end of the world, but you can see it from there!

I can never thank Ron Zuchelli, my high school football coach, enough for the job he did in selling me. You know, I made recruiting visits to Penn State and Pittsburgh, but both places thought I was too small. Hell, when I was a senior in high school, I only weighed 190 pounds. The big schools looked at me and said, "He's too small."

Naturally, it pissed me off. I was always a hothead. Yeah, I had an attitude that drove me.

Plus, try and figure this one out. Both Penn State and Pitt said my legs were too thin. What in the hell does that mean? I didn't tackle with my damn legs. You ever see Lawrence Taylor tackle with his legs? Hello? That still ticks me off. You ever hear a scout say a club passed on a player because his legs were too thin?

Plus, I had another problem. Schools all wanted to see film on me and we didn't have any film. Hell, we didn't even have Polaroids. I had to be sold through word of mouth to various schools. Coach Zuchelli really did a super job for me. Honest to gosh, I can't thank the guy enough.

COPPOCK: By this time, had you more or less put baseball on the back burner despite the fact that Lasorda had offered you that six grand to sign with the Bums?

BUFFONE: Honestly, I still wanted to play big league baseball.

Both sports were an option for me once I got to college. That's why Louisville became so attractive to me and my cousin Jerry. Jerry was a fabulous athlete; I mean just tremendous. He also played football and baseball. The guy had unlimited natural talent.

It's a shame when I think about what happened to him. He blew out a shoulder playing football at Louisville and that was it. Game over.

Sports can be so damn cruel.

It kills me to think about how much ability he had and what he could have been. The guy was absolutely the real deal.

COPPOCK: Let's backtrack for a second.

Give me the low down. Just how does Doug Buffone—with state, county, and local recognition as a primo linebacker and offensive center—wind up in the land of the Kentucky Derby and mint juleps?

BUFFONE: Several things happened. One, Coach Zuchelli drove us down to Louisville to get a look at the campus. I mean, he really was fighting like hell for us to get scholarships. How many coaches are gonna drive kids from the middle of nowhere in Pennsylvania to Louisville?

That's a 12-hour bitch of a round trip. But Ron did it, and both Jerry and I got our scholarships. We went as a package deal and it paid off. The school not only agreed to let us play both football and baseball, they *wanted* us to play both sports.

That made our decision really very simple.

People will ask me if I was pissed that the big guys, USC, Ohio State, and Alabama, didn't come chasing after me.

Screw 'em.

I never thought twice about it. I was really grateful to Louisville for giving me a shot.

COPPOCK: Did you need a full semester at the 'Ville to get fully acclimated to a new environment?

BUFFONE: No, not at all. Sure, there was a natural degree of anxiety. But I really wanted to get out in the world. I wanted to see if I could make something of myself. Keep in mind, I had a heck of a lot of belief in myself that I was going to be somebody. When I got to Louisville for my freshman year, I got the hang of things pretty rapidly.

Let me tell you something that really helped me. In high school, I played Class B football. We only had 18 guys on our team—*18 effin' guys.* We couldn't afford to lose any guys to injuries. Just 18 kids. We played schools that had three times as many players as we did. We were always matched up against Class A and Class AA schools. In other words, we had to learn to throw punches early and often. As a result of that, I wasn't lacking confidence when I got to Louisville. I knew from Day One that I wasn't in over my head. I had been an underdog and an overachiever all my life.

However, the first thing I recognized was that my wardrobe had to be adjusted. I needed to get a more preppy look to fit in with the other kids.

COPPOCK: Too bad I didn't know you then. How do you feel about raccoon coats?

BUFFONE: I hate raccoons. But, I've got to tell you a story about my old man. It just fits. Dad, from years in the mines, wasn't scrawny. He was a bull. His forearms, biceps, and his neck were all huge. I mean just huge.

It was time for me to step up physically, too.

So, after my first year, I came back and with a new body. I had beefed up. My weight went up from 190 to about 220. I was now a *man* on the football field.

So, what did my dad do?

He decided to test me.

He looked at me when I arrived at the house and said, "You think you're pretty tough now, don't ya?"

Then he had us lace on the boxing gloves.

I had a big senior year at Louisville, winning 2nd Team All-America honors. I was also chosen MVP of the Senior Bowl.

Growing up, my dad used to punish me by making me absorb blows. He never hit me bare-fisted. He always used boxing gloves. It was his old-school style of discipline. So now we go outside to duke it out and I'm pretty confident I'm gonna hold my own.

That was a mistake.

Dad kicked the shit out of me. I mean he just unloaded on me.

When he was done clobbering me, he said, "Do ya still think you're tough?"

COPPOCK: We have a hundred different ways we can travel at this point, but tell the house about the legendary bar fight you had and how your beloved head coach left you out in the cold.

BUFFONE: This was just hysterical. I mean, I still laugh out loud thinking about how that whole thing happened.

Try and follow me on this one.

I was with a girl in a bar one night and this guy comes over and asks her if she wants to dance. She very politely says no. Well, this son of a bitch isn't gonna take no for an answer. He kept asking and asking and I finally told him, "Listen, ya heard her say no a hundred times. Now leave her alone."

Well, now this guy starts in on me. He said, "Who's gonna make me shut up?"

I told him, "I am." Then I added, "Listen pal, I don't want any trouble. Just leave us alone, okay?"

That's when the fists began to fly and I mean this was the brawl in the hall. The place went up for grabs and it didn't end in the bar. Not by a long shot. It spilled out into the alley where my buddy said, "C'mon Doug, stand behind me. We'll fight 'em back to back."

I told him he was crazy. I wanted to fight leg to leg. In other words, I wanted to get the hell out of there. I didn't care if the other side claimed victory or not.

Shit, who the hell cares? Because by now, I didn't know if the babe I was with was still in the bar or three counties away. All I know is a guy just smashed a beer bottle against a wall and I'm thinking, "I'm gonna look like a busted catsup bottle!"

COPPOCK: I'm going to take a wild guess that you were given an official set of "bracelets" through the kindness and generosity of the Louisville police department.

BUFFONE: Damn right we were cuffed. We were taken to a local lockup, which didn't do a lot for my nervous system. I was half-drunk and I bragged to the cop that I was a Louisville football player and all he had to do was call Frank Camp, our head coach, and everything would be fine.

Boy, I was naïve. Or maybe stupid.

My coach was a character and a half. He spoke in this long pronounced Southern drawl. I can still remember Coach Camp telling me when I first got to Louisville, "Doouuuugg, you be suuuurre to stay outta trouuuubbllle."

Honest to God, that's exactly how he talked. He couldn't say a full sentence in under three minutes.

COPPOCK: So, did Frank Camp, the all-knowing Father Flanagan of your football program, get things squared away?

Did he come down in his pajamas and get you off the hook?

BUFFONE: No way in hell.

The cop called Frank up and I could hear them talking back and forth and he finally walked over to me and said, "I just got done talking with Coach Camp. He said he's never heard of you."

Never heard of me?

I spent the whole damn night in the joint singing, "Swing low, sweet chariot," while I clanged a Coke can off the cell bars.

I don't think I ever got around to, "Coming for to carry me home."

COPPOCK: Just how the heck did you make bail?

BUFFONE: Coach Camp came down the next day and got us out. In hindsight, he just wanted to teach us a lesson. He succeeded, believe me. One night in the joint can change your outlook in a helluva hurry.

COPPOCK: You've got to tell us about that guy who had the misfortune to walk into the wrong gym and meet the wrong fighter.

BUFFONE: Every football team always had guys who thought they could fight and the fact was, a lot of them could. But we had this one guy who was a little overmatched. The guy ran into that toughest guy in the universe.

After my first year at Louisville, this poor guy comes back with a busted nose and a black eye. He looked like he'd been hit by a truck.

So, I asked him what the hell happened. I figured he'd been rolled.

It turned out that this nut case had gone down to a local gym where a young Muhammad Ali, then known as Cassius Clay, was training. Somehow, this idiot wound up in the ring with Ali, who proceeded to do a number on the poor guy.

Here's what I've never understood about the sparing match this guy had with Ali.

What in the hell got him into the ring that day?

Ali wasn't that far away from winning the heavyweight title over Sonny Liston in February of '64. This damn fool had no business stepping into the same solar system, let alone the same building with Ali.

My God.

I guess the dumb sap must have insulted the future champ, maybe the greatest heavyweight of all-time. There is dumb and there is dumber! This jerk obviously put a lock on dumber.

COPPOCK: Your old man didn't have any dough. How much money did you take with you from home when you went to Louisville?

BUFFONE: My parents didn't give me a dime. They couldn't afford it and I didn't need it.

I worked as a Christmas tree grower my last three summers of high school. I made 60 cents an hour. I would just boil under that hot sun, eight to nine hours a day, shaping trees for people to use during the holidays.

I really hated the work, but it got me in good shape. It was hard labor, but at least it wasn't the mines. At least I could see daylight, for crying out loud.

The work made me strong. It set me up for my career in college and pro football. Believe me, after a full summer of shaping trees, there's nothing about two-a-day football workouts that were going to scare me.

Thank God for hard work. It's like a Porsche; there is no substitute.

chapter 5

The Old Man and His Young Genius

COPPOCK: The old-timers who follow Louisville's football team still gleam when you mention the name Doug Buffone.

Understandable.

Buffone was a three-year starter for the Cards at both center and linebacker and closed his career with 473 tackles. He was picked in the fourth round of the NFL draft by George Halas, but really, he was a George Allen selection.

Allen had a dual role with the Bears, serving the Old Man as both his top defensive coach and director of player personnel. He was grossly underpaid at around $19,000 a year. Allen left Chicago on bad terms with the Papa Bear when he accepted a job offer from owner Dan Reeves to become the head coach of the Los Angeles Rams following the 1965 season.

Halas was livid with his bright young football mind. In the Old Man's world, Allen's move without Halas' consent was tantamount to treason. Papa Bear eventually went to court to uphold the "validity" of his deal with Allen.

He won a very hollow victory and then, this is just so Halas, let Allen pack his bags and move to the West Coast. Papa Bear had made his point. In the mind of the NFL Godfather, it was a great win.

When I think of George Allen, two thoughts come to mind.

One, he had a nervous habit of licking his fingers constantly, and, secondly, Allen didn't see football as a game or a livelihood. He saw it as life and death. And that was on a Tuesday in June.

He told me more than once that, "Every time you lose, a little bit of you dies."

Jeez, the guy could have been Shakespeare or Al Pacino.

BUFFONE: It's really a funny thing. Allen drafted me and then he left town. You know, a lot of us wonder just what would have happened if the Old Man had retired after he won his last title in '63 and given the club to Allen.

O'Bradovich will tell you that the Bears would have won at least a couple more titles if Halas had stepped aside.

I hate to say it, but the game had passed Halas by and he had too many coaches who were really just friends. Nobody really knew why Sid Luckman (part-time quarterbacks coach) always seemed to have the Old Man's ear.

But he did.

COPPOCK: Let me tell you something about Sid—a lot of guys can back this up. Around 1980, the Old Man and Luckman had one of their frequent dinners. Papa Bear just adored Sid, and Sid knelt in reverence to George Stanley Halas. Shortly after this particular dinner, Halas wrote a very warm, glowing letter to Sid expressing his love for Luckman as both a man and a football player. The note was mesmerizing.

Sid loved to send copies of the Halas letter to friends. I had a copy. I know Kenny Valdiserri, the Bears P.R. chief, had a copy. It was really all over Chicago. I don't blame Sid for showing off his written "toy." He hadn't played in over 30 years, and like most of you guys, he yearned to get back in the pads just one more time. When Luckman saw that note, I truly believe he saw himself back of center "Bulldog" Turner on December 8, 1940, when the Bears clobbered the Washington Redskins 73–0 while really introducing America to the T-formation.

BUFFONE: I hear ya, but there were times with Luckman and the other assistant coaches that we as players frequently asked each other, "What the hell are we doing?"

I was drafted by the Bears in the fourth round and the San Diego Chargers picked me in the eighth round of the AFL draft. Now, this was at a time when the AFL was going all out to force the NFL to merge, so they were spending *big* money.

Halas offered me $18,000 my first year, but the Chargers were ready to pay me $30,000.

Think about that, $30,000 in 1966. That was a heck of a lot of money. You know if I'd had an agent I probably would have signed to play on the West Coast.

So, what did I do?

I took the offer from the Bears.

I told the Chargers, "Listen, I appreciate your offer, but I'm a cold-weather guy. I just can't play football where there's palm trees."

COPPOCK: You gotta be nuts! What do you mean you can't play where there's palm trees? Who says that?

BUFFONE: I did. I really meant it. The Steelers had a lot of interest in me as a hometown boy. They even indicated they might take me at No. 1. But I didn't want to play for them. Before Terry Bradshaw got to town, they were the biggest losers in the league. They were just awful.

You know, the Bears had a hand in Pittsburgh's revival—do you remember what happened?

Both the Bears and Pittsburgh were 1–13 in 1969. In fact, the Bears' only win was against the Steelers. So, the two teams had a coin flip to figure out who would get the No. 1 overall pick.

COPPOCK: The flip took place at a hotel in New Orleans. Ed McCaskey, Halas' son-in-law, made the call for the Bears. He chose heads. The coin came up tails.

Legend has it that Jack Griffin, a brilliant writer for the *Sun Times,* yelled out, "McCaskey, you bum. You can't even win a coin toss." I'm guessing it had to be said in jest because Griffin was really a classy guy. I can't imagine him seriously taking a pot shot at Ed.

The Steelers took Terry Bradshaw.

True story: When I first joined the Bears, some fans thought I was Native American. (photo courtesy of Getty Images/Bruce Bennett Studios)

The Bears then set the clock back 10 years. They traded the second overall pick *within the freakin' division* to Green Bay. Who the hell does that? Who trades the No. 2 overall pick in the damn division for God's sake? It shows you how out of whack the club was.

The Pack gave up three guys: Bob Hyland, Elijah Pitts, and Lee Roy Caffey. All three guys had two things in common: They were not going to change the face of the Bears or any other franchise in the NFL.

And they each had one foot in retirement.

It was a pathetic waste of a pick.

Meanwhile, nearly a generation later, in the fall of 1982, Buffone, after several years out of football, would hear again from Allen. George, who hadn't coached since he left Washington after 1977, had been hired to coach the old USFL Chicago Blitz.

Now, the Blitz had about as much impact on Chicago as a moth slamming face first into the Trump Tower.

George wanted Doug, and in classic Allen fashion, he was ready to overpay.

BUFFONE: I really liked Allen. He called me about joining the club and I said, "Listen, if I could still play, I would be with the Bears."

So, George said, "I'll pay you $300,000 a year to play for me."

I said, "Listen, I just can't play anymore." So, Allen counters, "I just want you to call the defenses."

The guy was persistent. I said no. I had other business interests and I knew I really had nothing left. Allen took me to a Blackhawks game and said at the top of his lungs, "You gotta play for me." I shot back, "No, I'm done. I haven't got a damn thing left. Twenty-two-year-old running backs are gonna run me over."

COPPOCK: Buffone made the right call. He really was out of fuel. In his final season with the Bears in '79, Doug could no longer play sideline to sideline. The kid who could fight off a blocker on the strong side and chase down a running back on the other side of the field just wasn't there any longer.

Father Time had come around to collect the tabs.

Buffone also had thriving business interests.

However, I always figured Jim Finks, the club's taciturn, chain-smoking general manager, would want to keep Buffone around as an assistant coach. Finks, a stand-up guy, loved guys like Doug, players who in theory overachieved. Jim was the rare individual who earned the right to be called a man's man.

Finks did a prolific job rebuilding a decimated franchise when he joined the Bears in '74, but by the close of the '81 NFL season, Halas had seen enough of Jim. Or, it could be argued, that Halas couldn't resist the urge to "reclaim" his franchise, the club that had earned its bone back in the '20s beating teams like the Hammond Pros and the Rochester Jeffersons when pro football garnered about as much attention as field hockey. Keep in mind, no one ever suggested that the Old Man had a pint-sized ego. Halas loved control. He thrived on control. The fact that his son Muggsy was able to convince the Papa Bear to step aside in '74 and let Finks run the entire football operation remains, to this day, a major football miracle.

Near the close of '81, I knew that Gary Fencik and Alan Page, two guys who commanded big-time respect in the Halas Hall locker-room, had sent a letter to the Old Man urging him to retain Ryan. Gary and Page weren't dummies. They knew incumbent coach Neill Armstrong was headed for the guillotine. Armstrong had about as much fire as Pee Wee Herman.

Halas claimed the letter from his defensive stalwarts was magnificent. Was the Old Man really all that moved? Did the prose of Fencik and Page really melt the Old Man's heart? Frankly, I have my doubts.

But it clearly planted a seed with George. Coach Halas was 86 years old, and I always felt he wanted to swing the bat one more time. In his own way, who could blame Halas if he felt the need to enhance his legacy before he left to "meet his maker"?

So Halas, without giving Finks the time of day, went ahead and re-upped Ryan to a fresh deal with a very healthy raise in salary. Honest to gosh, Finks never saw the move coming, but he sure as hell knew what the move meant. Halas was reclaiming at least a share of the driver's seat. Jim was so damn pissed he couldn't see straight.

That was step one. Here was the shot heard around the world. Early in 1982, Halas, without any input from Finks, hired his old sparring partner Mike Ditka to run the Bears. Once again, a letter was supposedly involved. Ditka, knowing full well that Armstrong was going to get axed, had written Halas a love note. It was a two-fold document.

Iron Mike was clearly asking the Old Man to forget his comments about Halas, "throwing nickels around like manhole covers," and he was pitching to become the next head coach of the Bears.

BUFFONE: You know Halas really wasn't fair with Finks. I really like Jim. He wouldn't take any shit. People would tell me during my years with the

I will always owe Hall of Fame quarterback Sid Luckman a huge debt of gratitude for his love and kindness.

Bears that I should have an agent. Maybe they were right. Maybe I did leave some money on the table, but I really enjoyed my negotiations with Finks. He would always call me and say (laughing), "Put a tie on, come down to the office, and we'll talk about your contract."

We never really slugged it out over money. I knew Finks respected me. I knew he appreciated old-school football and he always paid me what I figured I was worth.

Think about some of the people the Bears have had over the past 25 years and while you're doing it, look at the Green Bay Packers. Green Bay had Ron Wolf, Brett Favre, Mike Holmgren, Mike McCarthy, and Aaron Rodgers. The Bears have had guys like John Shoop, Mike Martz, Mike Tice, Frank Omiyale, and Jared Allen.

Christ, in 2014, Allen didn't earn a dime. You tell me what he did besides wave his arm trying to get fans into the game. He was pathetic. I'm sure the crowds wanted to tell him to shove it.

COPPOCK: You know when the Bears signed Allen, I said he'd be a bust. He was coming off the carpet in the dome in Minnesota. Now, he was going to be playing on grass. Plus, the next time Jared Allen stops the run I may ask the city to give him a parade up and down State Street.

BUFFONE: You know, this tells you something about the Bears. This club has not been cheap. Forget that shit. But all too often the club has been stupid. Listen, I don't have any gripe with Cutler getting that $100 million deal. I blame Phil Emery for not franchising the guy. At least with Cutler, you were investing in a quarterback; with Allen, you bought a used car business.

COPPOCK: There would be no football future with the Bears after Doug left the game. I have little doubt he would have been a tremendous defensive coordinator, but No. 55 decided to make the clean break. Buffone knew what sidekicks were making those days. He also wasn't the kind of guy to sit in a dark room, gazing at a projector, breaking down toss plays and screen passes.

Honestly, Doug's greatest strength, and this has got to be a byproduct of his youth in western Pennsylvania, was that he always saw life beyond the extra point. He truly knew football was an opportunity to carve out a career away from hip pads and team meetings.

Doug Buffone was always as tactical as he was tough.

chapter 6

NFL Primetime

COPPOCK: Buffone didn't join a bunch of junior varsity castoffs when he hooked up with the Bears for his first training camp back in '66. He joined a group of hard-bitten, nails-tough veterans.

Guys like Big Doug Atkins, O.B., Joe Fortunato, Bennie McRae, Rosey Taylor, Davey Whitsell, and Richie Petitbon weren't poster boys for Krispy Kreme. They were seasoned, bad-ass pros who'd won a title under George Halas back in 1963.

They didn't look on Sundays as a game. To them, it was their soul.

Mike Ditka, one of the 10 most complete NFL players I've ever seen, was also part of the action, along with second-year legends Dick Butkus and Gale Sayers.

The Bears, coming off a 9–5 season a year earlier, mistakenly believed they were a club that might be headed toward dynasty status. Instead, they were about to break fans' hearts from Waukegan to Michigan City, Indiana, with a free fall that went beyond epic.

As far as rookies went, these guys weren't big on welcoming parties. In those days, every new Bear got tested on a pass/fail. There was no in-between. They didn't give a damn about a fourth-round pick out of Louisville.

They did care that Buffone had just played for the All-Stars against Green Bay at Soldier Field in the long-gone, *Chicago Tribune*–sponsored College All-Star Game.

BUFFONE: I got to camp and I'm not intimidated but, you know, I'm nervous like any other rookie. So, who's the first guy I see?

Atkins.

He was 6'8" and while the Bears listed him at 255 pounds, he had to be closer to 290. The guy was a giant.

So, Goliath walks up to me and says, "Who the hell are you?" And before I could answer him, he raised a sleeve on my Ban-Lon shirt and said, "You got any muscles on those arms?

Christ, I didn't know what to say.

Guys used to tell me about Doug's martini drinking contests with Freddie Williams. Players would marvel that Atkins could down 20 martinis in one sitting.

The guy was from a different universe.

COPPOCK: I don't buy any talk about Gino Marchetti or Willie Davis or other great NFL defensive ends back in the '50s or '60s.

Atkins was Mount Rushmore, absolutely in a class by himself.

If sacks would have been recorded throughout Doug's career, I have no doubt he would have racked up at least 250. And mind you, Doug began his career during the days when the NFL was still running 12-game schedules.

The only guy who was in Doug's league was Deacon Jones, a monstrous pass rusher, who attended Mississippi Vocational College, an all-black school. The Deac, who made the head slap the most vicious weapon in pro football, never played football against a white guy until he joined the NFL.

Mercifully, years ago, the head slap was banned. God only knows how many guys Jones left punchy.

Trust me, Michael Strahan would have caddied for Atkins and Jones.

BUFFONE: You know, Atkins was just a piece of work.

It's my first year and we're running the "Halas Mile." The whole club had to do it and you had to get in under a certain time. Well, Atkins is just trotting along while the Old Man is screaming at him to get moving.

Finally, we get to a turn and Doug just runs off the track and heads toward the locker-room. Halas was livid. I mean, the Old Man was out of his mind.

You know, Doug liked to screw with Halas' head. So as he's leaving the track, he yells back at the Old Man, "Fuck you! I'm a football player, not a track man!"

Halas really drove everybody crazy when we played the Packers. Everything was doubled up. The assistant coaches felt the pressure along with the players. We called it "Packer Panic" week.

Christ, one time Halas stopped a practice and told everybody to "Get over here!" He said, "They're spying on us."

So, what does the Old Man do? He points to an airplane that was flying way the hell over Wrigley Field. It had to be at 30,000 feet. You could barely see the damn thing.

That was the "spy."

Guys couldn't believe it.

Atkins knew Lombardi just drove Halas out of his mind during the Green Bay weeks. Atkins loved to walk over to the Old Man and say, "Ya know coach, I think there's a guy up in section 116 in about row 18 who's looking at us. I think Lombardi's got one of his guys watching us."

Of course, Halas would then tell Atkins to go fuck himself.

COPPOCK: Ed O'Bradovich hasn't played a down of football in Chicago for damn near a half century. Yet, he remains an iconic figure in the Windy City.

O.B., a dynamically charismatic figure, earned his checks making life a car wreck for stars like Bart Starr, Johnny Unitas, and Roman Gabriel.

Ed generally led the nation in hitting QBs just after they'd released the football. If there was a rule to be bent, O.B. took advantage of it. The guy's killer instinct was never an issue.

For years at Cubs Park, there was a sheet on the east stands that said, "Go, Go, Ed O." It's odd, but I can never recall any banners praising Butkus or Gale. Bears fans just loved O.B.

You know, Eddie went to Proviso East in Maywood. The guy came off as a bona fide working-class hero. He also wasn't big on treating newcomers like Barbie dolls.

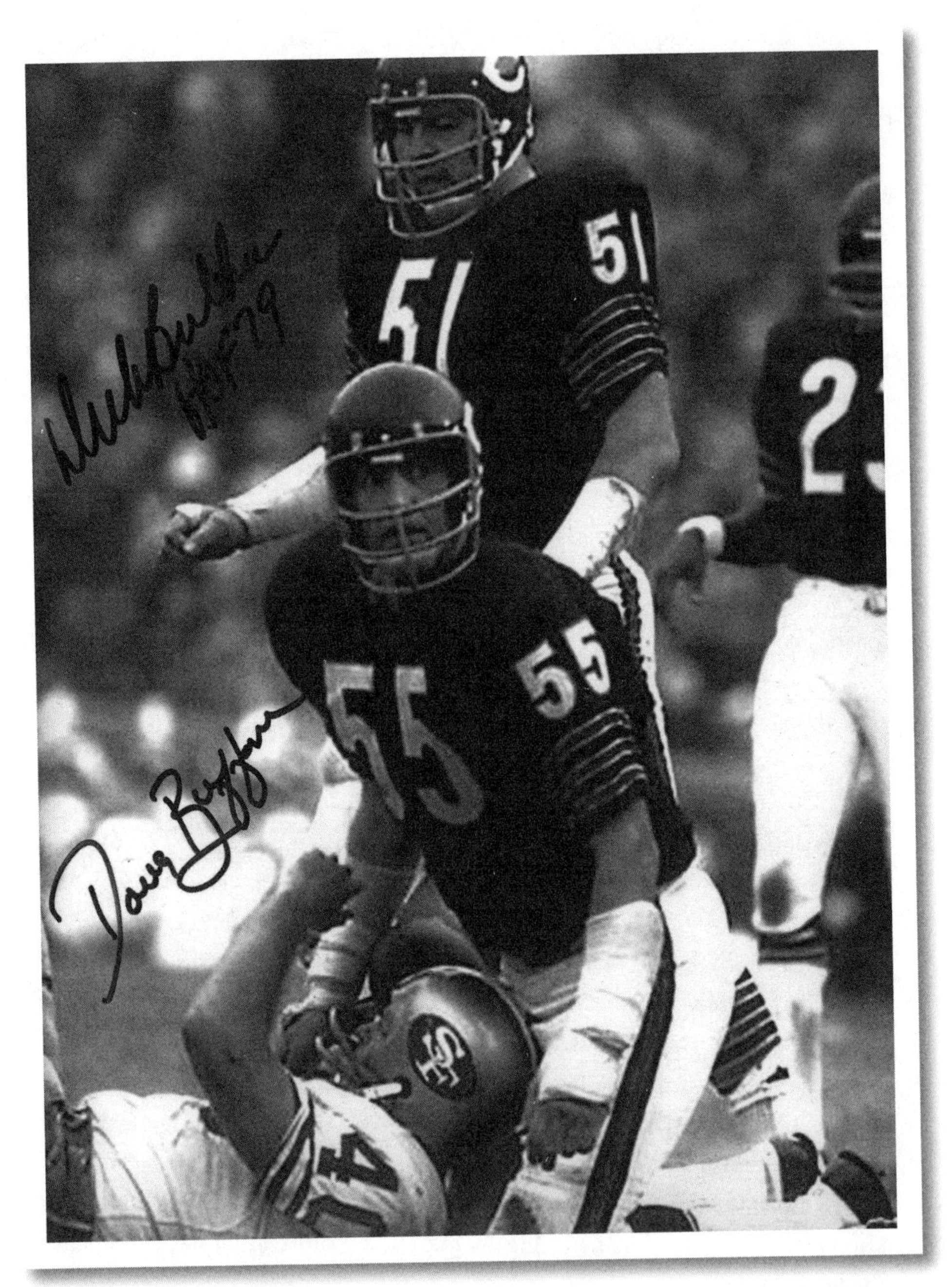

Butkus is doing what he always does—looking for anybody to hit. Dick and O.B. were the greatest teammates I ever had.

BUFFONE: I remember the first time I got a chance to play. Joe Fortunato got banged up, and I heard the Old Man yell, "Buffone, get in there." So I went running on the field to get in the huddle.

O.B., whose facial expressions could scare a serial killer, looked at me and said, "Hey kid, you got any idea what the fuck you're doing?"

You see, these guys were tough. They didn't give anything away. They made you earn respect.

In a way, O.B. reminds me of the first time I faced Lombardi. I knocked some guy out of bounds near the Packers' sideline and I kept rolling till I damn near hit the bench.

So Lombardi yelled at me, "Did you know Buffone in Italian means 'clown?'"

I got up and yelled back at Lombardi, "Shut up, you yellow-toothed asshole." It's probably a good thing they left my response off the Super Bowl trophy.

You know, when I was a rookie, Fortunato gave me the best advice I ever received. It was probably my first or second NFL game. Some guy held me and a back blew past me for about 12, maybe, 15 yards. When I got back to our bench, Joe said, "What the fuck happened to you out there?" I said the son of a bitch held me and the ref didn't call it.

Fortunato gave me this cold, dark stare and said, "Listen, pal, the next time that happens, kick the guy in the nuts."

What can I tell you? That was the game we played. I hear this crap from TV commentators today saying guys from my era couldn't play today. They don't know shit. I'll tell those jerks, "Yeah, Butkus, Gale, Jimmy Brown, Johnny Unitas, and Lombardi's Packers couldn't play today. No, there are one helluva lot of guys making $400,000 a year to work the kickoff teams today who couldn't play when I played."

I like Alshon Jeffery, the kid with the Bears, but his job is to run downfield, turn around, and catch the ball. Or if he doesn't catch the ball, scream like hell for a penalty. He knows d-backs have to lay off him.

Move him back 40 years. How would the kid have held up when guys in the secondary knew their job was to just pound the crap out of receivers when they didn't have the football? *Our guys couldn't play today?* That's such a crock.

Does that mean Walter Payton couldn't play today? I played with Walter for five years. Remember, when he broke in, offensive linemen couldn't hold the way they hold today.

COPPOCK: Your game was never the same when the league put in a rule—I think it was '78—that prevented defensive players from making contact with receivers five yards past the line of scrimmage. It was originally packaged as the "Chucking Rule." Now, it's whatever Troy Aikmen calls it.

BUFFONE: The game is painfully over officiated. Every time the referee goes under the hood to look at a play, the momentum just stops. Meanwhile, TV looks at the play involved from 11 different angles. You know when I played, we accepted things. The ground could cause a fumble. A receiver either had the ball or he didn't. You think we ever heard this crap about a guy "making a football move" to establish possession? Frankly, I liked it that way.

chapter 7

Big Abe

COPPOCK: How do you explain Abe Gibron in 100 words or less?

BUFFONE: (Laughing) The answer is you don't.

COPPOCK: The rotund former guard was named head coach of the Bears after the club finished a dismal 6–8 in 1971 under Jim Dooley.

How dismal?

The mighty offense scored *29* points over the club's last five games.

Trust me, Dooley's four-year run with the Bears was no picnic. Jim was a remarkably cerebral guy, who also had a fondness for the race track. If you were in the know, you knew there were times when Sid Luckman covered for Jim financially when he was in need of cash. That didn't make Dooley a bad guy—not by a long shot. Anyway, Jim had taken over the Bears after the 1967 season, when the Old Man coached his 40th and final year with the team he gave his life to building.

There was a consensus among the local media that Dooley might bring forth a "new era" with the Bears.

However, if you looked closely at Jim's roster during his tenure, there were usually glaring weaknesses at about 14 positions. In reality, Dooley could coach, but he was stuck with palookas. There were times, I swear, I thought the Bears were making draft picks off what they read in the *Sporting News*.

BUFFONE: So much for the consensus opinion, right? It didn't help Dooley that his two heavyweights, Gale Sayers and Dick Butkus, both suffered significant knee injuries during the time Jim was trying to call the shots. By '72, Dick on his good days was playing on one leg while Gale, sadly, after just 68 NFL games, was out of football.

As for Abe, he did have one thing in his favor with the Old Man.

Halas just loved Gibron's passion.

I think the old coach looked at Abe and saw a throwback to the days of Bronko Nagurski, George Trafton, and other legends from the '20s and '30s who stood in reverence of George Stanley Halas.

Now for the reality.

Gibron, a product of Michigan City, Indiana, went to four Pro Bowls as a member of those tremendous Cleveland Browns clubs under Paul Brown in the 1950s. He also had a tour with the Eagles before gravitating to the Bears in 1958.

Abe reported to camp pathetically overweight. He weighed 280 plus, but the son of a gun broke his back and won the everlasting respect of Halas when he worked his weight down to a solid 248 pounds.

The press conference the Bears threw to anoint Abe as their new head coach was hysterical. It made the WWE or Ultimate Fighting look like a bible study class.

Abe, being Abe, didn't meet the media in a sophisticated suit with an orange and blue tie.

BUFFONE: I'm not sure if Abe even owned a tie.

COPPOCK: He entered his coronation in an open-collared shirt, looking at best, completely disheveled. When some guy asked Abe how long his deal as coach with the Bears was, he announced, "I haven't signed a thing and we haven't even entered any long-term negotiations."

Next question.

As for football operations, Abe said, "I'll be in charge of everything on the field."

The literal translation: "The Old Man and his son, Muggsy, will tell me just who makes this club. My job is to keep my yap shut. Oh, and avoid Arlington Park."

That was the warm-up.

The frolics closed with the Old Man and Muggsy bum-rapping the *Sun-Times* and the old *Chicago Today* for what they said was irresponsible coverage.

That led to a minor shouting match between Halas Sr. and Bill Gleason, the outrageously funny but laconic columnist for the *Times.* Gleason was a frequent tongue-in-cheek critic of the Old Man. The two guys loved to spar with each other.

For want of a better word, their exchange on "Gibron Day" was "surrealistic." I gave Gleason a split-decision victory.

BUFFONE: Abe was really a piece of work. If he had one problem, it was that he wanted to be liked by everybody. But, sometimes you had to wonder what he was thinking. I remember after we lost a game to Detroit, he walked over to me and said, "Ya know we knocked nine of their guys out."

I asked Abe, "What difference does that make?"

They don't give you a win for the number of guys you busted up for Christ's sake.

Let me tell you what Abe was up against. He had some assistants on his staff who were just completely lost. One summer at training camp in Rensselaer, Indiana, one of Abe's guys calls me into the coach's office, pours us both a shot of Old Crow and says, "Our tight end is weird. I'm telling ya he's strange. He's not one of us."

I asked, "What the hell are you talking about?" The guy shot back, "I'm telling you the guy bats the other way. I'll prove it." So this psycho says he's going to check the guy's room before curfew. I told him he was nuts. He couldn't just barge into a guy's room unannounced, right?

Well, this guy does it and he finds panties and even a gun for Christ's sake. The funny thing is that the guy in question really wasn't a half-bad player.

Meanwhile, Abe pulls me aside about a week later and tells me about what the guy found. I told Abe after about 10 seconds that he could stop. I knew what was up. Poor Abe had a look of defeat and stared me right in the eye and said, "We got no chance."

If that doesn't sound like the Titanic, what does? Poor Abe, just like Dooley, was doomed from Day One. It's really a shame.

COPPOCK: Abe was a trip to the Fun House.

I was in training camp in 1971 or '72 when he had the players run the "traditional" Halas Mile. The Halas Mile, much like the Boston Marathon, had been around for years. Bob Jeter, the ex-Packer, almost died during the romp. He finished in something like 13 minutes.

About an hour later, Tim Weigel, who was writing for the old *Chicago Daily News,* asked Gibron if he was concerned about Jeter being so badly out of shape.

Only Abe could fire up this response, "I'm not worried at all about Bob Jeter. He's like I was. He's not a long-distance runner; he's built for speed."

Gibron had more trust in Buffone than he did in any other player he ever coached. Doug was Abe's sounding board. I think Gibron really saw Doug as an extended part of his family. I think Abe looked at Buffone and saw a son, a ballplayer cut from a special mold.

However, if you heard Abe talk about No. 55 in Halas colors, you had to wonder if Gibron actually knew who the devil was playing the "Sam" (strong side linebacker) spot for him.

Whenever Gibron referenced Doug Buffone, his message invariably came out as either, "Dub Buffoon" or "Dud Buffoon."

BUFFONE: (Laughing) Hey, Abe never claimed to be an English major.

COPPOCK: Gibron was non-stop laughs. In his first year as a head coach, the Bears played the Los Angeles Rams, a damn good team, to a 13–13 tie.

Now, in those days, long before dot-coms and the whole viral routine, maybe eight to 10 reporters would show up for one of Abe's postgame press conferences. You never saw any TV cameras. It was all about the print guys, the Associated Press, the UPI, the daily newspapers, and WCFL's ubiquitous sports reporter and pioneer, Red Mottlow.

Anyway, after this historic 13–13 standoff, Abe, after receiving about 30 minutes of congratulations from his drinking buddies from Michigan City,

Action coming my way. I can't let this Viking get inside me. (Photo courtesy of Getty Images/ Clifton Boutelle)

walked in and told the assembled throng, "This was a great Bear victory... er, tie."

BUFFONE: You know, Abe just loved to have Wednesday night cook-offs during training camp. He'd actually cook himself. Now, one night before one of the cook-offs, he invited me into his office at St. Joseph's and opened up his bottle of Old Grand Dad. We started to drink and we both got loaded.

The next day at practice, I'm just dying. I mean, I feel like hell.

So, what does Abe do?

He walked over to me and growls, "That'll teach you to stay out all night."

You know, back in '71, a year before Abe became head coach and he was just an assistant, our defense decided to try something new. Our offense was pathetic. The whole defense was just disgusted, really pissed off.

As a result, our defensive guys decided to become the offense. Butkus lined up at center and defensive back Garry Lyle was our quarterback. As we began to run plays, Abe walked up, frowned and asked, "What the fuck are you guys doing?"

I told him, "Listen, our offense can't score, so why don't you let us give it a try?"

Abe stood there dumbfounded. Then he told me to go fuck myself.

COPPOCK: He was a trip on and off the field.

In 1969, Hugh Hefner, the *Playboy* czar, opened up an "art theater" at Dearborn and Division. One of the first flicks Hefner brought to town was the controversial soft-core film *I Am Curious (Yellow),* which featured full-frontal nudity.

So, being a Renaissance man, I took a babe to see this flick. The movie is rolling along and about halfway through the film, I see this chubby figure in the first row.

He's snoring like hell.

I told my date, "Christ, that's Abe."

Anyway, the movie ended, the credits rolled, and the house lights went up.

So, I walked down to shake Abe back to reality and nudge the big guy out of his slumber. He looked up at me and his first words were, "Jeez, don't tell Halas I was here."

BUFFONE: Can you imagine what Abe would be like if he coached today and actually won some ballgames? The TV networks would have been all over the guy. He'd be a big-time star.

COPPOCK: He'd be Mike Ditka times 10. You know the NFL needs more Abe Gibron–type characters. Today, all these guys roam the sidelines in "home team" apparel, looking far more like high school cheerleaders than coaches on the highest level.

BUFFONE: We had a taste of TMZ even back then. Whenever I went to the old Playboy mansion with my teammates, we were always treated like royalty.

COPPOCK: That was before the media obsession with athletes we see today. Social media would love the big guy. He'd be on every night with his own reality show. Cookouts with Abe's Babes!

COPPOCK: Father Buffone, would you like to say anything in closing about Brother Gibron?

BUFFONE: Hey, I loved Abe, but there were times when he just didn't get it. You know, Abe was just so gullible.

One year, he called in Willie Holman, a guy who was really an underrated defensive end, and myself, to tell us he'd come up with an idea. Well, Willie and I both begin to roll our eyes as Abe told us he wanted me to be the leader of the white players and Willie was gonna be the captain of the black players.

What the hell? I told Willie, a guy with a smile a mile wide, that we had to screw with Abe's head. I mean we both had some ideas but we knew that it was gonna be a million laughs to bust Abe's chops.

Abe must have thought he was the second coming of Abraham Lincoln. He must have thought that he was hand-delivering the Emancipation Proclamation.

Race relations in this country weren't good at the time, but Abe said he wanted me to go back to the white players and Willie should meet with the black players so that he could make everyone happy and unite the team.

He wanted us to find out what the players "wanted."

I told Willie, "Okay, we gotta get serious about this and come up with a list of what each side wants here."

Well, I already know what all the guys wanted. They wanted Abe to cut the crap with the two-a-days and give us a break from the goddamn heat. Anyway, we met with our races and got together with Abe a day or so later and presented our lists.

So Willie goes to work on Abe. He said, "You got all this stuff for the white guys, but you don't have any hair products for the black guys."

Abe asked what the players wanted and Willie told him: "Afro-Sheen."

It works just like it sounds. You spray it on your hair to make it shiny and glossy looking, so it won't look dull. I still laugh today as I remember Willie trying to explain this shit to Abe.

But that's not all.

Willie's on a roll. He goes for the jugular. You know, we used to have regular mid-week cookouts, right? So Willie told Abe, "You've got Italian night, German night, and for God's sakes, French night, but you don't have an Afro-American night. My guys wanna know why the hell we can't have a Soul Food night."

I told Abe that white guys wanted double-ply toilet paper.

Christ, was he pissed off.

Abe's jaw just dropped to the floor. He yelled at us, "Get outta here, you sons of bitches."

God, that was funny.

Guys were always screaming about two-a-days, which wore us out. It was stupid. We were always beat up before the season even got started.

Well, one day we're going to hell and back and Abe tells us, "You guys think you have it tough? Look at those guys over there. They work out three times a day and ya never hear 'em complain."

So, who's Abe talking about?

St. Rita High School from back in Chicago.

We're grown men. This is how we earn our living. And he's screaming at us about how hard high school kids worked out.

I don't know, maybe the sun got to him.

Chapter 8

The Neanderthal Gene

BUFFONE: Football players aren't like the civilized world. We all have what I call, "The Neanderthal Gene." I know I had it. I couldn't have played the game for 14 years if I didn't have it.

But Dick Butkus was different.

I always maintained that Dick had two Neanderthal genes. The guy was super human; he hit like nobody alive. You know Butkus hated everybody, but he really couldn't stand Mike Lucci, the Detroit linebacker, and he just hated Vikings center Mick Tingelhoff. I mean, he just lived to hit Tingelhoff.

I remember the Vikings were just kicking our ass late in the year in a game that meant nothing. They must've led by 40 points. Or at least it seemed like 40 points.

In those days, guys didn't take a knee like they do today. So, we're late in the game with almost nothing left on the clock and they run a play. There's only a few seconds left and Butkus jumped up and screamed, "Timeout!"

I looked at Dick like he's nuts and asked him, "What in the hell are you doing?" And Dick just glared at me. So, what the hell am I gonna say?

So, as Minnesota is preparing to run another play, Dick called our defense, and then dropped back about eight yards and took a run at Tingelhoff. I mean, he belted the hell out of him.

And again he shouted, "Gimme a timeout!"

I said, "Dick, for God's sake, let's get the hell outta here. We're getting killed."

So, Butkus takes another run at Tingelhoff and whacks him again.

Then, he calls our last timeout.

This is all happening with 30 seconds left and we don't know what the hell to do. Neither did Tingelhoff. He was reeling.

You know, Dick was my roommate. He is one hell of a funny guy and people really don't know how intelligent he is. Hell, one time I saw him in camp reading Shakespeare. I'm not kidding.

I've always said that there should have been a sitcom built around Dick. He would have made Alex Karras (Mongo in *Blazing Saddles*) look terrible. Alex, the legendary Detroit lion, was funny, but Dick was much funnier. And as you know, Karras made a heck of a lot of money as an actor.

Dick made me laugh out loud when he did those Miller Lite commercials with Bubba Smith. Butkus just knew how to play to the camera.

COPPOCK: Did Dick ever bite another player?

BUFFONE: I don't know; maybe he did. But I am certain he bit someone. I remember it well. We were in a game when Dick brought a guy down and one of the officials went to get the football. All of a sudden, I hear this shout and it's the ref, white-faced and ashen, squeezing his hand.

Dick won't admit it, but ya know he bit the guy.

COPPOCK: That was Butkus. To him, rules were a waste of time.

BUFFONE: I still talk to Dick all the time. He's having a tough time with his legs. He called me the other day and said, "Christ, my leg gave out on me today and I fell into a bush." Think about that; Dick Butkus falls into a bush. You know the guy's in constant pain.

Butkus paid a big price to play this game. To say he played hurt is an understatement. He played when he should have been on crutches. The Bears overdosed Dick on cortisone.

I feel sorry for him and Gale. They deserved better. Jeez, those guys, as great as they were, never played in a playoff game. It makes ya sick. The damn Bears never surrounded those guys, Hall of Famers, with enough talent to play in a single postseason game.

The Bears should be ashamed! Butkus and Sayers both busted their asses for the Bears—and for what? What the hell did the club do for them? I'm telling ya the Bears should feel ashamed at how little they did for two of the greatest football players in NFL history. Who was a better linebacker than Butkus? Who had Gale Sayers' talent? The answer is nobody. The Bear didn't do crap for them.

Listen, Butkus had an attitude. His whole body said, "Don't fuck with me." There were guys on our own team who feared him.

COPPOCK: Speaking of great linebackers, Bill George is flat out one of the greatest football players in NFL history.

Like Doug, he played with the Bears for 14 seasons, earning All-Pro honors eight times. If he didn't invent the middle linebacker spot, he gave it a massive chunk of glamour along with Sam Huff of the New York Giants way back in the 1950s.

For the record, Huff couldn't carry George's jock. As good as Sam was, he was also a massive creation of the New York press.

Later after retiring from the game, Bill had a brief fling as a defensive coach with the Bears. One week, Coach George decided he needed to rev up Butkus, which didn't make sense because Dick needed revving up as much as Elizabeth Taylor needed another husband.

BUFFONE: Yeah, we were preparing for the Lions and Bill decided he needed to pump Butkus up, so he arranged to have a fake phone call from a guy who would announce that the Lions were going after him on Sunday.

For Christ's sake, every team went after Butkus.

But Bill wanted to especially motivate the entire team with this ploy.

So, I told Dick and our other linebacker, Ross Brupbacher, about what Bill had in mind. Butkus wasn't supposed to know Bill's plan, so he hid behind the lockers and listened in.

So, the call came in and George and some guy were talking about Lucci and how the Lions were planning to tear up Butkus. George came back in and said to Ross, "Are you gonna stand behind Dick Butkus?"

This was hilarious.

He is and was living, breathing ferocity. My guy, Ed O'Bradovich, putting the muscle on 49ers return man Doug Cunningham.
(Photo courtesy of Getty Images/Tony Tomsic).

On cue, Ross says, "He makes all the money on this club. Why should I stand behind him?"

Now Bill's pissed and so he asked me, "Buffone, are you gonna protect your guy?"

And, I said, "I agree with Ross, Butkus is making more money than any of us. Let him protect himself."

Bill George is aghast, sky-high pissed, that no one is defending our star player.

Dick jumped out from behind the locker and everyone had a big laugh—except for Bill.

Meanwhile, Dick is collapsing with laughter.

COPPOCK: In the game, Dick went out and busted up Charlie Sanders, who retaliated by knocking out one of your teeth.

It was how the game was played.

BUFFONE: You know the Bears haven't won a whole hell of a lot of games over the past 50 years or so, but God, they have turned out hitters in droves. Guys who just lived to lay the wood on other players. Butkus is obviously the top guy on my card but think about how vicious Dan Hampton was. What about a guy like Wilber Marshall? I never saw a linebacker that size clobber people the way Wilber did.

You know this may surprise a few people since Mike Singletary's in the Hall of Fame, but I think Otis and Wilber were more complete players. Look at Mike's career. He had Hampton and Mongo up front with Otis and Marshall flanking him. How could he miss?

But for a middle linebacker to come up big, he's gotta have support. Look at Urlacher. He was at his best when he was standing behind Ted Washington and Keith Traylor. That's just football.

Butkus? His whole mentality was I'm gonna leave you for dead. I hit you, you don't get up. You had to kill him to get him off the field. Late in his career when he just couldn't make the stops he'd made in his early days you knew it made him feel like hell. There were practices where Dick could barely walk but he still played on Sunday.

COPPOCK: I gotta throw this into the mix. You know I regret the fact that I never got to know Marshall. I'm not sure any media guys did get to know him. I'm not kidding. When I looked in his eyes, he was actually frightening. Wilber was so damn good that I really believed he never needed to practice. He always looked to me like a guy who could play 36 holes a day, Monday through Saturday, show up on Sunday, and leave half the Green Bay Packers in body casts. The kid was the very definition of the phrase "football player."

BUFFONE: Let me tell you about Doug Plank. I love the son of a bitch, but there were times he'd drive me nuts. I mean, I could talk about a hundred plays where he could have had picks, but interceptions didn't mean a thing to Doug. Really. He played to hit people. When he saw a receiver coming across the middle, he wasn't thinking "ball," he was thinking, "This guy is dead meat."

There were times he came back to the huddle when I asked him what he why the hell he took the man instead of going for the pick. Frankly, it was like talking to a wall. That was the way Doug was. He was a Pittsburgh-area kid. It was the only way Doug could play.

It's a shame Doug didn't hang in long enough to play with the '85 champions. Jeez, the Bears had great safeties, Gary Fencik and Dave Duerson, but Ditka would have had to find a way to get Plank on the field. The guy would have been a special teams kamikaze.

You know before games, Plank loved to bang our guys head to head with his helmet. Christ, he'd bang his head off the goal post or anything else that was tied down.

This is the truth: Plank scared me more than guys on other teams scared me. You see, it didn't matter what the hell the jersey color was. If Plank saw a chance to fire out, hell, he might knock out half the guys on our defense.

COPPOCK: Think about Todd Bell, the kid from Ohio State. There's never been a guy in the Chicago secondary who could hit like Bell, not Plank, not Dave Duerson, Mike Brown, not anybody. The guy was a pit bull disguised as a football player.

BUFFONE: Bell showed you how one play could absolutely demoralize a club. In that '84 playoff game between the Bears and Redskins, Washington was running the Bears off the field until Bell put a lick on Joe Washington. Bell just took him to school, creamed him. Joe gave up the ball and the Bears went on to win. If the Redskins had scored on that possession, the Bears just don't win that game.

Otis Wilson was another guy who could murder rival players. Otis had the perfect body to play football. He was big with a tremendous upper body. Plus, if you talked to Otis, you knew it was a waste of time to give him pep talks. The son of a bitch was ready to play on Tuesday night. Guys like Marshall, Todd, and Otis just scared the hell out of people. Football is about intimidation. Hey, we aren't selling used cars; we're hitting each other—goddamn hitting each other like hell.

COPPOCK: I remember one play where you just got caved in, handed your lunch. Tell the student body about that given moment.

BUFFONE: I know what game you're talking about. It doesn't matter who the hell we played; that's not important.

This is. Let me tell you what happened.

A guy from Green Bay—it was always about Green Bay—hit me so goddamn hard that my *balls* were in my throat. I mean, I couldn't breathe; I could barely stand up. But, here's the thing. I never conceded. I never let this bastard know I was hurt. It's like the gladiators in the Colosseum in Rome. We are gladiators. I couldn't let that guy know he got to me.

There is nothing worse than getting beat, but if you tell the guy, "Hey, great stick," or "Gee, you got me," you're admitting weakness. I never admitted weakness. Never would.

Chapter 9

Lion Tough (Say Hell to Charlie Sanders)

COPPOCK: Speaking of Charlie Sanders, he always looked as if his chest was ready to bust out of his Honolulu-blue Detroit Lions jersey. The "book" said Sanders packed just 224 pounds on his 6'4" frame, and maybe the book was on target, but here is what you have to understand about the former Lions tight end and card-carrying member of the Pro Football Hall of Fame: He was a wicked athlete who defined the phrase "complete player."

Don't let his gentle name fool you. Charlie was not a librarian and part-time girls' softball coach from Poughkeepsie. The more I watched Charlie over the years, the more I felt that he should have been raised in western Pennsylvania. Sanders had that brutal, small-town mentality that was so much a part of Buffone, Bill George, Joe Namath, and Jimbo Covert.

Point blank, Sanders would own today's NFL.

Hey, you know as well as I do that the league had embraced, absolutely sworn allegiance, to a "hands-off" policy with guys going downfield. That would have made Charlie, much like Mike Ditka or John Mackey, virtually impossible to defend.

Plus, you just don't find true tight ends in this pass-happy, made-for-TV league, ones who blocked with the authority of Ditka, Mackey, and Sanders.

I would like to thank Detroit's Charlie Sanders for my gap-toothed grin. (Photo courtesy Getty Images/Tony Tomsic)

Tight ends, save short yardage situations, have become, for the most part, glorified slot receivers.

BUFFONE: If Charlie played today, he'd be an All-Pro in a heartbeat. I put him on the same level with Ditka and ahead of John Mackey. Ditka was a helluva blocker, but Charlie was also really physical.

Mackey couldn't block as well as Charlie. Sanders was more complete than John. And you know Mackey was chosen to the NFL's 1960s Team of the Decade.

COPPOCK: You know, the Lions really haven't won a damn thing since they beat the Cleveland Browns 59–14 back in December 1957 to win their last NFL title. Detroit has far more often than not followed an abysmal pattern for 57 years.

That's not a slump. That's a descent into hell with no heaven in sight.

In August, hopes in Motown are always hovering at 35,000 feet. But traditionally by September reality sets in, and three weeks before Halloween the club's fan base is consumed with the NFL Draft.

Yeah, the one in April.

Granted, the Lions have had some truly gifted players over the years. Texas gunslinger Bobby Layne, hostile middle linebacker Joe Schmidt, and an elusive butterfly named Barry Sanders were all monuments to achievement.

All were Bears-breakers.

Now, class take note.

When Charlie Sanders joined Detroit in 1968, the Lions won 13 of their next 15 games against the Bears with the big guy on the Detroit roster.

BUFFONE: God, were they that bad without Sanders? And that damn good against us with Charlie?

You know, Detroit at the time had some damn good players. Guys like Mike Lucci, Lem Barney, and Mel Farr had strength, savvy, and speed. Lucci, not coincidentally, was from western Pennsylvania.

Sanders was another tough guy who did his talking with his blocking and physical toughness. I never did trash talking, either. I knew I had a job to do and I went about my business. Talking always distracted me and Charlie was also kind of a quiet guy, too. As a result, Charlie and I never talked. We just belted the hell out of each other every chance we got.

When we played the Lions, our main goal was to stop Sanders. It was a bitch. The guy wouldn't give an inch.

COPPOCK: Meanwhile, big picture time, Lions history was best defined by Matt Millen, their former GM, who brought the word "ineptitude" to a new level, followed closely—and cluelessly—by former head coach Marty Mornhinweg.

Don't tell me you've forgotten about Marty's sideline genius?

For heaven's sake, the guy went a bedazzling 5–27 in two years as the Lions' field general. Plus, he came up with one of the greatest tactical errors in NFL history—an error so absurd you can be forgiven for guessing that Marty guzzled his pregame "breakfast."

In 2002, while Soldier Field was undergoing renovation, the Lions faced the Bears at Memorial Stadium in Champaign. If you can explain just exactly why our boy Marty did this, trust me, you're way ahead of Marty and me.

The two clubs battled 60 minutes to a draw and the Lions then won the toss going into overtime. Mind you, a dog-tired Detroit defense had given up two scores late in the fourth quarter to give the Bears the OT shot.

So, the Lions received, right?

Not a chance.

This is how you earn a career winning percentage of .156 as an NFL head coach. Marty, despite having a terrific kicker in Jason Hanson, elected to take the wind.

Take the *what?*

The crazy son of a bitch turned down the ball, a move which was as hapless as Justin Bieber doing stand-up comedy.

With great delight, the Bears marched 43 yards downfield and set up Paul Edinger to knock down a field goal that gave Mr. Personality, Dick Jauron, a 20–17 win.

BUFFONE: What Marty did was nuts. He was trying to think outside the box. He must have wanted to show his guys that he wasn't regimented. That's how coaches get themselves beat.

A coach can just kill a team.

You know with Marty, he's gonna be forever linked with that overtime folly.

You know on defenses, all it takes is one guy to screw up and he kills ya. I know. Believe me, I know. I've been there too many times.

COPPOCK: Following his disastrous George Armstrong Custer epiphany, Mornhinweg said, "Knowing the outcome of this game, I wouldn't do it again."

Great, and since we are on the subject, the Ford Motor Company would never have offered the American public the Edsel either. If you don't know about Edsel, you probably don't know about *Leave It to Beaver.*

But back to Charlie Sanders.

His hands were baby soft, which belied the fact that he was a wicked, downfield blocker. I can still see Charlie blowing up Bear defensive back Garry Lyle's knee with a wicked-as-hell downfield block at Soldier Field.

The court has also determined that Sanders was also the man responsible for Buffone needing major dental work.

BUFFONE: I know what you're talking about. I just fell asleep on the play. It was really my fault. I was chasing a guy down and the prick put a forearm right in my face. He just nailed me. I never saw it coming. He got under my face mask and chipped three of my teeth.

One of them had to be removed. Thus, the gap-toothed grin. God, my nerve endings were exposed. The rest of the day, every time I hit somebody, it just sent a jolt through my entire body.

It was absolute hell.

Later, after my career was over, Dr. Stewart Dunn gave me permanent false teeth.

And no, Charlie didn't say a word to me about what happened. He really didn't have to. Hell, I don't think he knew what he'd done to me. Listen, with today's rules, he would have been thrown out of the game. I mean he cracked me right across the mouth.

But we played a much different kind of football back in those days. Honestly, I really didn't think much about what he had done to me until I got back to the huddle. That's when Butkus looked at me spitting blood and said, "Watch, this guy is gonna pay."

Just a couple of plays later, Dick caught Sanders over the middle and drilled him; I mean fuckin' creamed him with a shot to his chest.

COPPOCK: Charlie has admitted over the years that the blow was so decisive, so powerful, that he really didn't feel it. The Butkus blast simply left him numb.

BUFFONE: (Laughter) I've always wanted to believe that Dick clobbered Sanders just for me, but that's probably not true. Knowing Butkus, he would have decked Sanders anyway.

COPPOCK: Knowing Butkus, he would have decked Halas if he thought it would win a ballgame.

Chapter 10

Tragedy in Detroit

COPPOCK: It was a day drenched in unspeakable grief. A journeyman football player lost his life.

Forty-four years after the fact, reality and disbelief are still waging war. The score hardly seems worthy of mention.

It was the darkest day in NFL history. I know. I was in the stadium.

For the record, on October 24, 1971, the Bears upped their seasonal success to 4–2 with a 28–23 win on an overcast Sunday over the Lions at old Tiger Stadium. I can still hear the screeching sound of an ambulance departing the ballpark en route to a local hospital.

I remember Ed Stone, a terrific football writer for the old *Chicago Today,* telling me on the press box elevator, "I think that guy's dead."

Eddie was right.

BUFFONE: It was so unexpected. No one said anybody was going to die. That's not part of the deal. You know if you go into military combat that you might die, so you deal with it. To be honest, I really didn't know who the guy was.

COPPOCK: There were probably a fair share of Lions fans at the old venue on Trumbull and Michigan Avenues who shared your sentiment. They really didn't know who Chuck Hughes was, either.

Hughes was hardly an NFL glamour boy. He was just a guy from Philly who'd played a few years as a backup wide receiver with the Eagles before moving on to the Lions. Chuck had the misfortune to collapse and die on the

A moment so devastating I still sometimes wonder if it truly happened. The Lions' Chuck Hughes dies on Tiger Stadium field during our 1971 game with the Lions. (Photo courtesy AP Images)

field during the final minutes of the contest. His demise wasn't due to any physical contact. Hell, he wasn't even supposed to be in the ballgame.

The only reason he'd entered the show was because Larry Walton, who'd caught a TD pass from Greg Landry earlier in the afternoon, had pulled up lame. Shortly before his heart gave out, Hughes had made his first grab of the year, a 32-yard reception from Landry that moved the Lions into "plus territory."

BUFFONE: I do remember that when Hughes ran back to the huddle before he collapsed; he seemed like he was very winded. He was puffing rapidly, sort of like a steam engine. But, Christ, who had any idea he was suffering a heart attack?

Again, we all think we're gladiators in this game. What happened to Hughes just wasn't supposed to happen.

COPPOCK: Two plays after the Hughes catch, Landry threw the ball to tight end Charlie Sanders near the Chicago goal line. Sanders, normally sure-handed, dropped the ball. While most Detroit fans were groaning over the Sanders' miscue, I've got to figure that only a handful of people immediately noticed that Hughes had collapsed face-first near the 20-yard line.

BUFFONE: This is where Butkus comes in. Dick was standing over Chuck with his arms up in the air. A helluva lot of people thought Dick was "show boating" or "posing."

That's crap.

Butkus was waving like a madman towards the Detroit bench for the medical guys to come out and take care of Hughes, who was turning purple. Butkus really caught a lot of heat for what was a "friendly" gesture. He got a ton of hate mail the rest of the year. There were actually people who were calling him "Killer."

It really upset Dick terribly. The guy was ferocious, but he also had a big heart. The hate mail just gnawed away at him.

You know, I can still see two things when I think about that event. The first is the Lion's trainer pounding like hell on Hughes' chest, trying to revive him. Two, when they carried Chuck off the field, his arm was dangling off the stretcher like a broken wing.

I think that's when it really hit us that this was the worst.

COPPOCK: There were only 62 seconds left on the clock when Hughes went down. On a sunless day marked by a steady drizzle, the 54,000 fans in the ancient ballpark sat in stunned silence, absolutely deafening silence, as they witnessed the only death in NFL history to take place on a gridiron.

All that was really missing was a priest. The scene was beyond horrifying.

The Bears were winning football games and for a team that had gone 1–13 just two seasons earlier, they had every right to be happy. Bobby Douglass had shown signs of maturity, throwing TD strikes to George Farmer, a kid from UCLA who never made full use of his God-given talent, and Bob Wallace. Douglass also carried the ball in for another score.

The Bears were two games over .500 and actually in the race in the NFC Central.

BUFFONE: We really didn't know how to react in our locker-room. There was a very eerie feeling, a strange feeling. I mean, who in their wildest fuckin' dreams thought a guy would die on the field?

COPPOCK: The Bears' charter flight back to O'Hare was hardly a joy ride. There was an occurrence that seemed to question reality.

A flight attendant got on the speaker and went into a long congratulatory speech to the Bears on their win over Detroit. She had no idea there was little cause for joy. I can't blame the young lady for her celebratory attitude. She was on assignment and this was back in the days when "stews" treated passengers like human beings instead of so many pieces of cattle.

Maybe, the girl only spoke for 35 seconds, but given the circumstances, it seemed like two hours. I remember that some guy in the back of the plane finally yelled at her to "shut up."

Honestly, I don't recall who it was. But I do remember that Buffone, Butkus, and O.B. were all sitting together at the rear of the craft.

BUFFONE: You know the Detroit press didn't do Dick any favors. There were guys up there who went out of their way to bash Dick about what had happened. Butkus was an easy target. He was arguably the best pure player in the game and the Lions' media loved to build up the rivalry between Dick and Mike Lucci, the Detroit middle linebacker. Butkus just fuckin' hated Lucci, while Mike knew that he was never going to be as good as Dick. Nobody could be.

I don't think the true reality of what had happened hit us until around the middle of the week.

Again, it all went back to the fact that as football players, we believe we're invincible. If you don't think like that, you may as well wave goodbye.

You're toast—yesterday's news.

COPPOCK: If the flight attendants remarks were ill-timed, defensive back Ron Smith, a tough kid, came up with a comment that made you wonder if he'd had his bell rung three times during the ballgame.

Smith hopped on the mic and said to the club, "I just caught Mr. Halas in one of his rare moods and he said if we win our next three games, he'll let us wear bell bottoms! You dig?"

A guy dies and this moron is excited about being Sonny Bono. Ed Stone looked at me. I looked back at him and both our expressions were of complete bewilderment.

The plane landed in Chicago.

There were no TV cameras to face. No horde of dot.com writers looking for quotes about the momentous tragedy. This was long before the Bears became a 24-hour-a-day, 52-weeks-a-year proposition.

Seven days later, the Bears beat Dallas at Soldier Field 23–19.

Life went on.

BUFFONE: I swear, the defense had to be on the field for over 80 plays. Honest to God, I'm still not sure how we won.

COPPOCK: Dallas was the apex. The Bears dropped six of their last seven games. The offense went straight to hell. What appeared in October to be a joy ride ended as a season best forgotten, a season of despair for several reasons.

And one in particular.

Chapter 11

Sweetness and Today's NFL

"If everything seems under control, you're just not going fast enough."

—Mario Andretti

COPPOCK: I suppose we could apply those words to Walter Payton.

Doug, it seems hard to believe that Sweetness has been gone for 16 years. You knew the guy a hell of a lot better than I did. To me, Payton was at once a brilliant player, emotionally vulnerable, cocksure, insecure, a tad egomaniacal, a little uncertain of his surroundings, and, last but not least, arguably the greatest player in NFL history.

BUFFONE: I could talk all day about Walter and what he did on the field. He just played his guts out and competed for years on mediocre teams before Jim Finks, the old Bears GM, began to surround him with talent.

But, let me tell you a story about Walter in the locker-room that was just hysterical. Odd, but hysterical.

The guy was crazy about dogs. He just loved 'em and he would frequently bring his dogs to practice. One day, he showed up with one of his bad-ass dogs—I think it was a Rottweiler—and after we got done working out, Payton brought the damn dog into the locker-room. Really, it seemed a little strange but, you know, that was just Walter being Walter. He actually did it all the time.

Anyway, Bob Parsons, our punter, a damn good one, came walking out of the shower and he was buck naked. For whatever reason, Walter's dog snapped and bit Parsons right on the ass.

I mean right on the ass.

Now, Bob is screaming like a madman, so Jack Pardee walks over to me and asks, "What the hell is going on with Parsons?"

I told him, "Payton's dog bit him on the ass."

And I mean, it wasn't a small bite. There weren't just a handful of teeth marks. The damn dog actually chewed flesh right out of Parsons' ass.

COPPOCK: Does this story have a happy ending?

BUFFONE: Not really.

Later that night at about nine o'clock, I decided to call Parsons at his home. When he picked up the phone and said hello, I started going "Woof… woof-woof." I didn't wait for Bob to say anything, I just hung up the phone.

Jeez, was Bob pissed. He was seeing double.

And no, Walter didn't stop bringing his dog into the locker-room.

COPPOCK: Payton was always jerking around. Did he ever get you involved in any of his pranks—I mean real killers?

BUFFONE: You know, Walter would do things that just made you laugh till you dropped. We were in camp at Halas Hall one year and there was no air conditioning, so I brought my own unit from home. I went to bed and the following morning, there's Walter sleeping on the floor in my room.

On the goddamn floor!

I said to him, "What in the hell are you doing here?"

Payton looked at me nonchalantly and said, "It was just too hot upstairs, so I came down here."

He also had a fixation with firecrackers. Walter just loved the suckers.

He grabbed me after practice one day and told me to follow him to Fred Caito's room. The next thing you know, I'm standing outside of Fred's room with Walter up on my shoulders. He took out an M-80 and lit it right by Caito's window.

Well, the window just shattered.

Payton and I ran back to my room like a couple of kids and locked the door.

COPPOCK: I should have a better read on this because I was in the Bears locker-room after they cakewalked over New England 46–10 in Super Bowl XX back in '86. A couple of Payton's teammates have told me that Walter was so distraught that he hid in a hotel closet when the Bears got back to the team hotel.

Why?

Because he was pissed off that he didn't score a touchdown.

Mike Ditka can give out all the excuses he wants, but allowing William Perry to score a TD over Walter was a criminal offense. Mike knew exactly what he was doing when he had the Fridge carry the ball for a score while Walter, who was all the damn Bears had to cheer about in the late '70s into the early '80s, stood on the sidelines in bewilderment.

Payton didn't realize that this was just vaudeville. It was show business.

BUFFONE: The way I heard it, Walter began to cry and hid himself in a closet in the locker-room at the Superdome.

I have some thoughts about that game and about what Mike did. I think Ditka figured, "This is a blowout, people are turning off their TVs, so let's give them a big dose of showmanship."

COPPOCK: Let me jump you for a second. Jerry Vainisi, who was tossed out by the McCaskeys as the club GM a year after the Bears won the bundle, told me this years ago.

On the morning of the "Perry draft" in '85, the Bears had a solid gold chunk of in-house turmoil. Personnel man Bill Tobin and Ditka both wanted Perry, while Jerry and Michael McCaskey believed that using a first-round pick on Perry was nuts.

Finally on the morning of the draft, Vainisi and Ditka arrived at Halas Hall at the same time. Jerry said he told Mike he could choose Perry, but he also made it clear that if William was a bust that the mistake was all on Ditka.

So, the Bears went ahead and took the Fridge at 22 in Round 1 out of Clemson.

BUFFONE: Here's my thought. Ditka began to think that he had invented Perry. I mean who the hell had ever seen a 300-pound player carry the football?

But, in reality, Bill Walsh had trotted out Guy McIntyre, an offensive guard, as a running back against Mike when the Bears got blown out by the 49ers at Candlestick Park a year earlier.

COPPOCK: That damn McIntyre could play. People forget that he went to five Pro Bowls and played on three Super Bowl winners. Bill Walsh trotted Guy out deep in the fourth quarter of the '84 NFC title game when the Niners manhandled the Bears 23–0. I don't think Mike will forgive Walsh for that move if he lives to be 90.

BUFFONE: So, think about the Super Bowl. What was the score when Perry got his TD carry?

COPPOCK: The Bears were clinging to a 37–3 lead.

BUFFONE: Now, ask yourself this question: If New England had been leading the Bears by seven, or even trailing by seven, do you honest to God think William Perry carries the football?

Not a chance in hell.

Walter Payton, the guts of that franchise for so many years, a guy who missed just one game in his entire career, scores that touchdown.

COPPOCK: I've always had this feeling about what Mike did. He had the biggest of the big stages. His stock was soaring. This was his way of showing the nation and two-thirds of China just how damn good he was at his job.

Jogging with Walter Payton in Chicago's Streeterville district. Thank God we weren't running up No. 34's legendary "hill."
(Photo courtesy of AP Images/Charles E. Knoblock)

Keep in mind, when Mike took over the Bears in '82, a ton of people thought Halas had gone nuts. Plus, Mike, in his own way, was telling his fellow coaches, "Look at me, I just one-upped Bill Walsh."

BUFFONE: You're leaving out the coup de grace.

The NFL was evolving. Hulk Hogan pose-downs were becoming a way of life in the league. The entertainment era was headed toward high gear.

That Bears-Pats Super Bowl was getting painfully dull. The Pats couldn't play dead. New England was a four-round fighter in the ring with Marvin Hagler, so Mike injected showmanship.

He went with Perry. He kept the TV audience.

Walter didn't know how to grasp it. All he knew was that he was in his 11th season. That's 11 years and he never took a play off. I knew the guy played till he dropped. His dedication to the sport was unmatched.

COPPOCK: NBC's Dick Enberg did come up with a great line when Perry crossed the goal line. He told his audience that they had seen a Super Bowl first...a touchdown scored by an appliance.

BUFFONE: You know I still love pro football, but the game has become as much show business as it is a sport. Look how the TV networks built up Richard Sherman, the cornerback from Seattle going into the 2014 Super Bowl?

This is a league that survives and thrives. It deals with head-trauma issues, post-concussion syndrome and the league still continues to rake in money.

(At this point, Buffone reached for a large, manila envelope that explained his injury benefits in the event he began to sink into the mental dungeon of hell. That situation had already grabbed former teammates such as Mike Pyle, Doug Atkins, and Dick Evey, a damn good defensive tackle. Sadly, all are mentally incapacitated. It's become common knowledge that a number of '85 Bears are suffering from the physical and mental trauma the game inflicted upon them.)

BUFFONE: I've been reading this pamphlet about concussions, and if I get hit with Parkinson's disease, or just go completely wacko over the next 10 years, my family will collect $3.5 million.

I worry about my memory (Coppock's note: Buffone is remarkably sharp) and I also know the NFL doesn't give money away. Roger Goodell, NFL Commissioner and noted class clown, wouldn't pick up a tab at White Castle.

You can't fool yourself either. I can't workout anymore the way I'd like to. I can't break a big-time sweat. That does piss me off.

Last year, I was jogging at a pretty good pace and tripped on one of those little risers you find in sidewalks. I really took a bad fall. My elbows, a shoulder, my neck, and my face all got messed up. Dana had to take me to the hospital. I was more embarrassed than anything else.

The worst part of it was dragging myself back to our house. I just felt stupid.

You know when I played, the game was more real in the sense that we didn't promote ourselves. When you scored a touchdown you handed the ball to the referee. For God's sake, act like you've been there.

Who was that guy at Cincinnati who used to have that stupid dance?

COPPOCK: Ickey Woods and his immortal "Ickey Shuffle."

BUFFONE: Yeah, I wanted to tell him to shove that shuffle right up his ass.

COPPOCK: We've got to get Larry Wolfe into the offense. Let me fill the house in on Larry. He's a down-to-earth guy who's been your accountant for years. His list of clients would make virtually any other accountant in North America drool. It's an endless parade of big-time jocks, entertainers, and business heavyweights.

Anyway, Larry told me a yarn about you making a Boxcar score on a Walter Payton jersey.

BUFFONE: It's true. This is really something I never dreamed would happen. After I'd left the Bears, I still went over to the team's facilities to work out every once in a while. Now, one day I forgot to pack a t-shirt which is, of course, dumb. So what did I do? I began to rummage my way through this garbage pile of game-used jerseys. I mean, the son of a guns were just lying in a trash can.

The first jersey I grab is a game-worn Walter Payton jersey. I put it on, work out, go home, toss it in one of my dresser drawers, and forget about the damn thing.

But the story is just beginning. A card company—you know one of those memorabilia places—finds out I have the jersey. They offer me $10,000 for the thing, which I accepted in under three seconds. The company tore the jersey into little pieces and sold it as part of a trading-card deal.

COPPOCK: God, that rags me. When Jim McMahon opened his second-rate restaurant over at Armitage and Sedgwick after the Bears won the Super Bowl, I got a call from one of his guys asking if I could "lend" Mac some memorabilia. I gave them, you're gonna die, Dick Butkus' rookie year jersey. You tell me what that piece was worth.

Here was the deal. I told them the jersey had to be framed and locked into the wall. And, I also said, if the joint tanked I want the jersey back immediately. Well, the place died an instant death, so I drove over to get the Butkus piece. Guess what? No jersey. I have never seen it. Hell, that could have saved me a year's tuition for my daughter, Lyndsey, at DePaul. The jersey had to be worth $25,000.

BUFFONE: Hey, you got screwed. It happens. I've been there.

COPPOCK: Let's move on, kid. Here's where the game is so dramatically different. Let's go back to 1967.

Suppose you're playing the Packers and you beat Forrest Gregg, Green Bay's Hall of Fame right tackle, and you sack Bart Starr. Now, if you go "Hollywood" and start "shooting pistols" at Forrest Gregg or get up and pound your chest over Starr, you tell me what would have happened.

BUFFONE: Gregg wouldn't have gone after me, but one of his players would have. You see when I played in the NFL, there was a code of honor. You beat me, that's fine, but you don't run it up and you don't show me up.

Guys in those days wouldn't stand for it.

COPPOCK: Here's how the whole racket has changed. In '68, you guys beat Green Bay at Lambeau Field 13–10. Gale Sayers ran for 205 of the toughest yards you could ever hope to see, while Mac Percival drilled a free kick field goal from midfield to give the Bears the win.

It remains the *greatest* football game I've ever seen. It was just punishing. It was like Ali-Frazier in Manila.

If that game were played today, the company man, ESPN's Chris Berman, "Mr. Hype," would say the game was "boring."

BUFFONE: Here's what really pisses me off big time. I'm watching a game on TV and some no-name defensive back nails a wide receiver over the middle. The guy drops like he's been shot and there's the DB standing over him like Brutus gloating over Julius Caesar.

That's just crap.

I get so furious that I want to jump through my TV screen.

I gotta believe this all got out of hand when guys like Billy "White Shoes" Johnson and Mark Gastineau, with his sacks, began to catch the glare of the TV cameras.

COPPOCK: Hey, I hold myself, in some small way, accountable.

You remember the '85 Bears–Green Bay game up north?

Mark Lee ran Walter Payton into the Bears' bench and later Ken Stills, the Packer defensive back, nailed Matt Suhey with a forearm shiver about five seconds after a play had been whistled dead.

I ran with those two items for five successive nights.

Why?

Because I knew listeners were intrigued, infatuated by the violence and the out and out cruelty involved.

Hey, what the hell does this league have to sell besides violence, gambling, licensed apparel, and fantasy football?

I laugh when the NFL says that gambling is a danger to pro football.

BUFFONE: Yeah, the NFL thrives on gambling—and I don't mean Vegas-type gambling, I mean the guy who bets through his bookie down the street. Really, who's gonna watch a late game between the Jets and Miami if they haven't got something down?

The answer is: not many people.

Gambling and Howard Cosell made *Monday Night Football.* It gave the degenerates an extra night to try and square up.

You know, thinking about Walter and what he meant to the Bears just made me think of something that I really get upset about. You know what it is?

I'm sorry, but I get so sick and damn tired of hearing sportscasters say that guys back in the '60s and '70s couldn't excel today.

That's such crap.

COPPOCK: Anybody who tried to tell me Doug Atkins couldn't play today should have their head mashed with a wrecking ball. Then, they'd know what it was like to play across from him.

BUFFONE: Good God, if Atkins played today, he'd have to be banned. The guy was impossible to block.

That goes for off the field, too.

We were playing in Los Angeles early in my career and I had gone down to the hotel restaurant to sip coffee at about 6:30 in the morning. Now, the restaurant faced the lobby. I noticed that there was this tiny figure darting from column to column in the lobby.

Finally, it dawned on me—it's the Old Man.

It's Halas.

He's in the damn lobby trying to catch guys who busted curfew.

Well, Big Doug arrives at about 7:30 AM. The guy had been out all night. I mean, you can tell he's feeling no pain. So, Halas came out from behind one of the columns and started whacking him with his hat. Halas is yelling, "You son of a bitch, that's gonna cost you $7,500."

Atkins looks back at Halas and yelled at him, "You don't fuckin' pay me $7,500!"

Now, here's what's odd.

Our huddle smelled like a brewery that day.

Four or five guys had been out with Doug and the funny thing about it is, all these guys played liked they'd been tucked in bed at seven o'clock the night before.

I seriously doubt if Halas ever collected from Atkins. Those two guys had a love-hate relationship, but the Old Man knew he couldn't push Doug too far. Atkins was just too damn valuable.

I'll be honest. Sometimes when O.B. and I are doing our postgame radio show, I get burned up and really pissed off because I see the kind of stupidity that reminds me of what I went through. Hey, I respect guys like Brandon Marshall and Alshon Jeffery, but what would they have done with the lack of rules we had 40 years ago? There were no five-yard restraining zones. Guys got up in press and beat the shit out of wide receivers.

And, if you weren't targeted with the football, defensive backs could turn you into a punching bag.

COPPOCK: On the final Sunday of the '63 season, the Bears had to beat the Lions to win the Western Division. What you're talking about reminds me of that game.

Visualize this. In the fourth quarter, Detroit's Gail Cogdill made a catch right in front of Bennie McRae, an ultra-physical defensive back. After Cogdill made the reception, Bennie actually picked him up and slammed him on the frozen turf at Cubs Park. I mean, slammed him.

If that happened today, a "guardian angel" like Joe Buck would be on Fox-TV screaming for McRae's head.

There was no flag. There was no penalty. It was just the way the game was played.

Here's my point. The game is more violent today because of the increase in speed, but it was a much rougher game as recently as 20 years ago.

BUFFONE: You know with the radio job, there are times, I probably shouldn't get mad, but I can't help it. Plus, the Score isn't paying O.B. and I to be Boy Scouts. I called out Shea McClellin the first time I saw him. I knew damn well he was never going to be a defensive end.

I always tell it like it is. I wasn't a plumber for 14 years. I played in the goddamn NFL.

chapter 12

Doug Plank: Blonde and Bloody

COPPOCK: Stop the music! Doug Plank can't be 62 years old. The blonde-haired missile who played on three Big Ten title clubs with Woody Hayes at Ohio State can't be headlong into his so-called golden years!

The kid with the baby face who won the hearts of so many Bears fans isn't allowed to fight a losing battle against Father Time.

Right?

Plank should be allowed—by law—to remain 25 forever. Doug always looked like the kid next door with the big grin who should have ventured to Hollywood by bus to become an actor. God knows, Plank has the rap down to a science. No. 46 can talk your ear off.

I have little doubt he could put on a better act than Arnold Schwarzenegger. Plus, I'd bet the rent he'd do better box office than the former Governor of California's recent films have done.

But the kid from Greensburg, Pennsylvania, is 62 years old and he works out regularly. You have to figure he's still a physical razor blade, though Plank admits, "I can't run anymore, which is alright, since I really don't want to." Doug Plank carrying an AARP card? I never would have dreamed that would take place.

Meet Doug Plank, hitter. Down the road, you'll meet Doug Plank, racquetball player.

BUFFONE: Plank admits that he doesn't have any idea how many concussions he suffered during his NFL career. He's said, "When I was dizzy and didn't really know where I was, I had a solution for that—I'd hit somebody head on. You know, helmet to helmet."

COPPOCK: That's not shaking the cobwebs; that's obliterating them. Let that be a lesson to all you moms and dads out there as you dress little Tommy for his Pop Warner League game.

Plank really shouldn't be a chapter; he should be a book. The guy played football like Joe Frazier threw left-hooks. Am I allowed to say that as a hitter, Plank was a Caucasian version of Jack Tatum, the venomous Oakland Raider? Now, a lot of people would argue that Tatum was a superior football player to Plank. I would agree that Tatum was simply one of the most complete NFL jocks I've ever seen.

It's a crime that Jack's not in the Pro Football Hall of Fame, and I have no doubt he would be if he could have brought himself to apologize for the paralyzing blow he put on Darryl Stingley.

As hitters, Plank and Tatum are 1 and 1a. Both, forever Buckeyes and warriors after Woody's own heart.

I have memories galore when it comes to Plank, but there is one date that sticks out, head and shoulders, above the others.

The Bears were playing an early season Monday nighter in 1980 versus Doug Williams and Tampa Bay at Soldier Field. The Bucs sent Jimmie Giles, their massive tight end, right up the seam into Plank territory. As the ball arrived, Plank hit Giles with a shot so brutal that Giles dissolved like a drunk falling out of Butch McGuire's at 4:00 AM.

I can still see Williams running downfield, getting in Plank's—and the official's—face when, in his haste to arrive there, he actually tripped over Bears linebacker Bruce Herron and lost his helmet.

No, there was no penalty on the play, but Plank was later smacked $10,000 by the league, which was big-time dough 34 years ago. Hey, Plank was only making round $80,000 at the time.

The Mayor of Mayhem and the Mayor of Rush Street: with Doug Plank and then–White Sox voice Harry Caray.

"You know I wasn't supposed to play in that game," Plank told me. "I can't lie... I did certain things so I could play that night and when I saw Giles I just knew I had a shot."

Plank calls it a "shot." The NFL of today would call it a beheading.

Plank admits years later that he appealed the fine and met with the NFL hierarchy in New York to plead his case. He had argued with the league, "I was medicated and really wasn't supposed to dress," so the brass lowered his tab to $2,500.

You know Plank was a great guy but, jeez, did he snap on the game face. He's told me a couple of times that when he'd see former Buckeyes before he played games, he'd always tell them, "Listen, I like you. I really like you. But when the game starts, I hate you. You aren't my friend."

Frankly, I've always bought the George Halas approach to postgame handshakes.

The Old Man didn't believe in them.

Halas' theory was very simple. Shake hands with the rival coach before the game and forget the "nice guy" act after the ballgame.

Halas told me that the losing coach was going to be ticked off, so why bother to try and play nice at midfield after you've had your head knocked off?

BUFFONE: I never got into postgame handshakes. I never goddamn helped another player off the ground. What are we doing? Are we celebrating the Fourth of July? Are we all gonna share a group cheeseburger?

Let's get back to that stuff later because I wanna give you my thoughts on God and football, but I gotta talk about Plank and my racquetball experience with a guy, who was, and I'm trying to be kind—I mean this in a nice way—walking on the edge of insanity. Really, you never knew who the hell Doug was gonna hit.

He was always on my ass to play racquetball. I used to blow him off, I'd say, "Doug, I don't like being on a football field with you, so why would I want to be stuck on a small little court?"

COPPOCK: I know you're gonna give in. You're better than even money to eventually say yes.

BUFFONE: Of course, I did. Jeez, did I pick the wrong guy. I knew going in that something bad was bound to happen, and it did. Really, the Bears should have posted a sign that said, "Playing racquetball with Plank is downright stupid or hazardous to your health—maybe both."

Anyway, if you know Doug, you know he isn't gonna take no for an answer. So, one day in Lake Forest in '78, he tells me, "C'mon, we'll play a nice soft game, just break a sweat and have a few laughs." Plank doesn't play for laughs. He wouldn't play miniature golf for laughs, believe me.

That's when I should have told him to take the next train out of town.

Get ready, here's the punch line. I'm serving and I toss a nice soft lob off the wall. Remember, this is going to be a nice friendly game and we're just gonna break a sweat, right?

So Plank goes for the ball and instead hits me right in the face with the goddamn racquet. I'm on the deck and we've been playing for, maybe, four seconds. My lip is bleeding. I've got blood coming out of my mouth. There's blood all over the court.

Now, Plank is jumping up and down screaming, "I'm sorry Doug. I'm really sorry." Christ, I think he was ready to call in a clergyman.

Freddie Caito, our trainer and the guy who treated my body like it was the Hope Diamond, runs over and asks this profound medical question: "What the fuck happened?"

Anyway, Freddie sewed me up. I wasn't mad at Plank. I was mad at myself. You know Doug played football the same way he played racquetball, or anything for that reason. It goes back to my point about Plank and interceptions. That just wasn't his world. In his world he just wanted to level guys. He lived to bust rib cages.

COPPOCK: Amen. Just imagine if Plank played today. He has that long blonde hair and he's blessed with a million dollar smile. Chicks fantasize about him 26 hours a day. The TV networks would make him millions in side money. At least, I think. There's just one minor problem. The Doug Plank who played in the '70s into the '80s couldn't be the same player in today's NFL.

Hell, 46 would be flagged 11 times in the first quarter. Buff, this game the NFL showcases today just isn't the NFL you survived for 14 years. In many respects, I find that very sad.

BUFFONE: The first time I saw Plank on the field I told our coaches, "This guy has gotta play." He was one helluva player and one helluva teammate.

chapter 13

'Roids and Uppers: the NFL Diet

"And though she's not really ill, there's a little yellow pill... She goes running for the shelter of a mother's little helper."

—The Rolling Stones.

COPPOCK: If you're scoring at home, the Stones anthem to instant gratification was released in 1966, the same summer that Doug Buffone began his 14-year tenure with the Bears.

In Buffone's rookie year, he found several ways to rev up his motor and cool his engine. He didn't need any lessons on how to get sloshed.

BUFFONE: Listen, I wasn't getting amphetamines from some undercover janitor. This was a Sunday-morning ritual, upfront and professional. I remember our team physician used to walk through the locker-room before the game with the pills on a giant tray. Guys took as many as they wanted.

COPPOCK: Nice buffet: chicken, pasta, pancakes, uppers.

BUFFONE: The amphetamines played mind games on you. They made you think you were playing better than you really were. But they obviously did give you a boost.

COPPOCK: Was Halas aware of what was going on?

BUFFONE: Sure he was. The Old Man knew. The whole damn league knew. Every club had a bundle of guys who were taking the stuff. I actually stopped taking amphetamines my third year as a Bear.

Listen, the Old Man wanted his best players on the field at all costs. So the heat was on the doctors to keep guys playing. It's always been that way with this game.

COPPOCK: Now, just to clarify here, uppers, downers, and "juice" didn't just become part of the NFL culture 10 years ago. They've been around, I swear, since the late '40s into the early '50s.

BUFFONE: But just where does the Hippocratic Oath fit in? You put your faith in a doctor that he's got your best interests in mind, right?

We took the amphetamines before the game and after the game, we took Darvon. That brought guys down and also relieved some of the pain we felt. Darvon made you a little bit drowsy. But you were still on a high from the game, so you really didn't feel the true effects of the drugs. My God, so many of the players needed them though.

Once, before a ballgame, the doc was late arriving for a ballgame. He got there just before kickoff. Guys were going nuts waiting for their yellow pills. Finally, he showed up and almost got trampled. There were players who felt lost without the uppers.

That was the reality of the NFL.

COPPOCK: Back in the '60s and into the '70s, the Bears never practiced on Monday. It was an off-day. A few guys might show up to have aches and pains treated, but essentially, guys spent Mondays recovering physically and mentally. And, for the record, sobering up.

BUFFONE: Now imagine this. Guys were taking uppers before the game and Darvon after the game. But we're not done yet. Most guys in those days went out and got drunk after the game. We'd drink all night.

So by Monday, you could hardly get out of bed. It's true because guys had gone through too many highs and lows. Their bodies were busted from the medical rollercoaster.

Players were getting high, going down, getting loaded and trying, of course, to get laid. Finally, after my second year, I decided, "Fuck this, I'm not gonna take the stuff anymore." I'm telling you I went through a helluva withdrawal.

I was climbing the walls I wanted the stuff so badly.

COPPOCK: Maybe Buffone could have continued taking the little yellow pills, but if he had, there's no way on God's Earth that he would have played 14 seasons. The highs and lows would have been too extreme. The toll on his body would have shut him down.

Doug hung around the league as long as he did because had above-average football intelligence, didn't make mistakes, and spent his off-seasons as a "workout warrior."

And book it, he was the good soldier despite the listless atmosphere of losing. He couldn't stand a lot of the hapless mistakes the Bears were making with personnel decisions, but he kept his mouth shut.

You have to wonder about the kid who became a very cosmopolitan figure in Chicago carrying the thought that a single misstep along life's way might lead him back in Yatesboro, P.A., carrying a lunch box.

Anybody who thinks fear doesn't motivate football players is nuts. Fear is the NFL's greatest form of motivation.

BUFFONE: Steroids messed a lot of guys up. I never got involved with the stuff, but cortisone also leveled a lot of players.

Jeez, during his last few years in the league, Butkus was living on cortisone. You know football is all this win-one-for-the-Gipper stuff, but we had a different take on it. We used to look at the doc and ask ourselves, "What the fuck is he doing?" We called him Zorro.

He was just a puppet for George Halas.

We were playing a game in San Francisco one year and I had a bone spur on my ankle. I was in agony. But I wanted to play and I played my ass off. I went ahead and got cortisone. I didn't know that stuff weakened your tendons. I learned in a hurry.

In the first or second quarter, I got hit and my tendon on the bad ankle just caved in. You know, it really was such a different era because we all lived in excruciating pain. It seems nowadays that a player comes out after a play, grabs some Gatorade, and gets toweled down after a 20-yard gain.

No sweat.

I used to get to the ballpark early before games and smoke about a half pack of cigarettes before the kickoff. But there's more to the story. I usually had two cigarettes waiting for me at halftime.

I had so much Stickum on my hands that I could just reach out with one finger and grab both cigs at one time. No wonder Fred Biletnikoff is in the Hall of Fame.

Our coaches would be walking around yelling, "We gotta do this, we gotta do that," while I'm just draggin' away on my cigarette saying, "Yeah, yeah, I hear ya."

chapter 14

Training Camp Wars

COPPOCK: Go back to the good-old training camp days in Rensselaer, that little country town 80 miles from downtown Chicago. A village so quiet, so docile, that it made Mayberry look like midtown Manhattan.

BUFFONE: I remember there was one bar in town that had this sign that said, "No dogs, no cats, and NO CHICAGO BEARS."

What can I say? I guess some of our guys got a little too rowdy there one night. Listen, that was Rensselaer, our summer training camp. It was something you loved and hated all in the same day, sometimes in the same minute.

COPPOCK: Ah yes, Rensselaer, the pride and joy of Jasper County, Indiana, so tiny that it needed an overdose of Red Bull to qualify as a sleepy metropolis. The quiet village of about 5,000 folks has become almost mythical over the years, a town that housed St. Joseph's College and scarcely little else, save the Bears.

The old timers, BWP (Before Walter Payton), still romanticize about the place, especially after three drinks. Sure, they remember the two-a-days in pads, and a blazing sun that seemed to be running at 212 degrees, or damn close to it.

BUFFONE: With humidity running 110 percent. Was that before guys started talking about the temperature humidity index?

Me and Sweetness having a good time at a press conference. (Photo courtesy of AP Images/Charles E. Knoblock)

COPPOCK: Even in December, if it was 31 degrees in Chicago, you always had the feeling it was still 94 in good-old Jasper County.

BUFFONE: Baked Bears. Sweat pouring off us. God, we roasted.

COPPOCK: But you guys also remembered that they worked out the kinks and shagged the off-season pounds on the same turf that Sid Luckman, "One Play" McAfee, the bulldozing Rick Casares, the indomitable Bill George, and the fleet-footed Willie Galimore (the most underrated back in NFL history), utilized to go through the breakdown process for the regular season schedule.

The old-timers still laugh at the eccentricities of Halas and his successors, Jim Dooley and Abe Gibron. Abe was, in fact, the "Round Mound of Rebound," long before the nickname was hung on Charles Barkley. They laugh about the hijinks, the long days on that sweltering practice field, and busted curfews.

I wish to hell every Bear fan, from eight to 80, could spend just one day on a summer afternoon in Rensselaer.

BUFFONE: The truth is that the food at St. Joe's was already terrific. We may have played like crap, but the food at camp was championship caliber.

COPPOCK: Life in Rensselaer could be mundane, beyond drudgery. Buffone remembers going to the Jasper County Fair a couple of summers just to see a guy who actually swallowed frogs. Rensselaer, endless cornfields and a guy who swallowed frogs, you're right, who needs the French Riviera?

BUFFONE: Speaking of animals, how the hell do you explain this one? One night, I came back to my room and there was no door. Some guy, I swear it had to be Dick (Butkus), used lighter fluid and burned down my damn door. Butkus always denied it, but I just know it had to be him.

Or it could have been Bobby Douglass.

No, it had to be Butkus.

You know when Dick is trying to tease you or rib you, he's got that grin that just tells you he's getting a leg up on you.

My roommate was Ross Brubacher. I told Bru, "Now, that the door is gone, they're coming after us. This is gonna be like the O.K. Corral." I had an idea that the worst was yet to come. Ross and I hung up a bed sheet, so we'd at least have a little privacy, but that didn't stop some guys from just nailing me.

I'm asleep a couple of nights later and I wake up with a raccoon on my chest. I mean, who in the hell does that?

I didn't know if the sucker had rabies or if he was gonna bite my head off. I just took a swipe at the raccoon, which actually looked like an oversized rat, and I knocked it against the wall.

Now, the raccoon wants a piece of me.

We're going head to head. He's clawing at me and I'm swinging for the fences. This wasn't some guy in a bar fight; this was a wild animal. I didn't know what the fight rules were because, you know, raccoons don't have rules.

I hammered him across the room. He finally escaped, I thought, through the window.

Escape hell—he came back at me, the little bastard. I could feel blood on my arms, but there's no way I was gonna quit. If he didn't want the window, he would get something else.

I grabbed him by the head and spun him upside down and back again and then flung him hard against the wall. He screeched and started to attack again and I drop kicked him out the open window.

God almighty.

I'm lucky that I wasn't chewed apart.

My guess is that the damn beast was left by some yahoo that lived south of West Virginia. You know some middle-of-the-woods guy. We always had a few guys like that on our roster.

COPPOCK: You had enough problems in training camp to worry about without a raccoon being at the top. The all-encompassing, omnipotent presence of George Halas was always in the air. Even if the Old Man wasn't in Rensselaer, guys could sense that the NFL czar back in his West Madison

Street office was looking over their collective shoulders. The watchful eye of Halas, 324 career wins to his credit, was always very tangible.

Even after the Old Man was retired, you still felt his presence with that pronounced jaw and his arms folded across his chest, knowing he was somehow peering into St. Joe's and wondering which one of his employees might be the next guy who would rip up the San Francisco 49ers or the Baltimore Colts—or the next guy who would turn up late at curfew.

His eyes were everywhere, watching you guys, making sure in his own strange way that you walked the straight and narrow.

BUFFONE: I only got busted once for blowing curfew. I skipped out with a bunch of guys after bed check. We drove up to the Indiana Dunes to get loaded. The Dunes was a pretty good drive. It had to be about 50 miles from camp, maybe more.

We got back later that night and "Silver Bullet" sees us. Bullet was the Old Man's security guard. I don't know what the hell the guy's name was. Bullet drove us nuts. He was always all over the place. The guy should have worked for the CIA or the Nixon White House.

That night, he went through the parking lot and began touching the hoods of cars to see which ones were warm. Naturally, he found mine since I was one of the guys who drove. I figured the club would fine me, but instead, they made me run...run till my tongue was dragging—and this after I'd already gone through another set of two-a-days in full pads. I nearly vomited I ran so damn much.

Actually, I would have been happier if I'd just been fined. It would have been a helluva lot easier.

One year, we had a going-away party to celebrate the end of camp. After seven weeks at St. Joe's, we were all dying to get back to Chicago. There was no "air" in Rensselaer. If you saw a tree, you ran like hell to get under it. The place was the Amazon rainforest.

One year, we had a party to celebrate the close of training camp.

The Bears, or maybe the staff at St. Joe's, carved a big "C" in ice to help us celebrate. Everybody let their hair down a little bit. I mean, we just had a great time.

So, what happens to me?

I go back to my room about an hour after the party and there's the flippin' "C" right on my bed, which melted and soaked it in water. My bed looked like Lake Michigan.

COPPOCK: You deserved a water bed endorsement.

BUFFONE: I don't know who the hell did it. I guess I never will. One of life's mysteries.

COPPOCK: Right up there with the chicken or the egg, Greta Garbo and the Sphinx.

chapter 15

Game Day

COPPOCK: Explain what it was like to play in the 1960s and '70s NFL. Your Sundays drenched in cruel reality, it was still in many respects a game played by bad-ass outlaws. The league was still built around "Take no prisoners." Flags were rarely thrown. A booth review would have been unthinkable. Christ, Halas might have punched out the booth reviewer.

BUFFONE: I used to vomit before every game. It was something I had to do. If I didn't barf, and this may sound gross or even stupid, I'd just stick fingers down my throat until I did.

It was as much a part of game day for me as getting up at 6:00 AM and reaching for a Marlboro. Vomiting, cigarettes, and tons of coffee—the recommended breakfast of champions.

It was how I got psyched up.

When you're an NFL linebacker, you don't read the *Wall Street Journal* and eat soufflé. You get into kill mode. I was getting ready for battle. It's blood, bruises, and breaking people, not Frisbee tossing in Lincoln Park or backgammon in Naperville.

I knew I was going out to get hurt and hurt others like the gladiators in *Spartacus.*

COPPOCK: God, I loved the sultry Jean Simmons.

BUFFONE: I hear you, pal. Nobody had to tell me about what I had to do to get ready. This is the NFL, not the real world. You had to think outside the box and the box was non-stop violence. Our fans loved to put on Bears caps, go to a sports bar, and scream obscenities like they were on the field with us.

In reality, they would have lasted about one play and been taken by ambulance to the emergency room at St. Luke's. You can't imagine the brutality out there.

It's beyond intense.

COPPOCK: Hence, the vomiting.

I've got to get you together with Glenn Hall, the legendary Chicago Black Hawk Hall of Fame goalie. Glenn was notorious for ralphing before games. In fact, Bobby Hull always told me guys figured that if Glenn didn't vomit, he wasn't ready to play.

BUFFONE: Understand this. On game day, there was so much going through your mind...you're worried about assignments, screwing up, and what the other team was going to do. I think when I barfed, it was just my way of cleansing myself, so I knew I was ready to play up to the level of ultimate survival.

It's also why I had such a hard time sleeping.

I used to get so wound up the night before kickoff that sleeping was damn near impossible. How can you relax knowing in a few hours you'd be throwing your body into a cement truck?

COPPOCK: Joe Fan and roughly 97 percent of the working press has no clue what your game is really all about.

You know when I got a feel for your game?

The first time I stood at field level back in the late '60s to experience just how crushing the hitting really is. My God, the screaming, the guttural grunts and the groans of physical debilitation go on every play. On TV, the game looks as harmless as an afternoon lunch with Queen Elizabeth and her rat pack of do-nothings.

BUFFONE: We were anything but spayed out there. We were rabid. That's the game—take it or leave it. Every hit could break a leg, an arm, or a career. Think Gale Sayers, Darryl Stingley, Joe Theismann....

COPPOCK: Explain the impact. What did the brutality feel like? I mean really feel like?

BUFFONE: Run full-speed into a brick wall and after you pick yourself up, do it again.

And again.

And again.

Until you're ready to collapse.

Then do it again.

Let me tell you what really pisses me off to this day. I had a brother, Sammy, who went to Vietnam. When he came back, people would walk up to him left and right and say, "I know what you went through over there."

Bullshit!

You don't have a frickin' clue what he went through. You weren't there. You didn't have to go into combat knowing any second you could take a sniper's bullet or worry about the Viet Cong, land mines, "toe poppers," napalm, bamboo torture, or Agent Orange, for starters.

My brother Sammy was the real hero in my family.

I was a football player and I won't be diplomatic. I was a hero to a lot of Chicago people, but Sammy was a guy who said if I have to leave here in a box, so be it.

That's guts. The guts of a man who was willing to throw away his education to fight for what he believed in! That's a hero. I don't want to listen to people who think they know what war is about. They haven't got a clue.

You tell me who the hell the hero is? I really get very emotional and almost have to fight back tears when I think about what Sammy did. In fact, I do get tearful. The guy, my brother...he had guts. He was a red-blooded hero.

People think they know what football is like, too.

I haven't played in over 30 years, but I still get guys who walk up to me and say, "Gee, I know how tough it was out there for you."

No, you don't. No chance.

Football is individual and collective cruelty on a 100-yard field. In a way, we were trained to be like soldiers. We had to cope with painful defeats. We're taught to accept excruciating pain. Guys who can't handle the injuries are over

Jim Finks earned my everlasting respect during his tenure as general manager of the Bears.

and out. No matter who we are, All-Pro or all-loved, on any given play, we are as disposable as a Kotex pad.

They could carry us off the field and run in a fresh body in a heartbeat. If you can't come back from your injury, go find another job. If your knee is shredded, your brain gets concussed, or your hip has been displaced, you're yesterday's news.

You're done. This game is a business. Perform or go open a yogurt shop.

You're coached to nail the son of a bitch on the other side of the line, and you're taught to take a hit, absorb the punishment, and never show weakness. You show weakness and you're dead. Word spreads like wildfire in the NFL. There are no secrets.

If you falter, your career dies. You can be the player of the week and be gone by the end of the following week. There is no security; there are no guarantees. You are forced to be Superman until you can barely walk.

Then you're a loser.

Lombardi had the balls to say it: "Winning is everything."

It's the cruelest career in sports.

And game day is its weekly memo.

COPPOCK: That reminds me of that helmet-to-helmet collision you had with Eddie Marinaro, the kid from Cornell, who swore up and down that he should have won the 1971 Heisman Trophy. In the pros, he was on the bench doing most of his talking.

In fact, I would dare say far more people knew him from his role on *Hill Street Blues* than from his days with the Vikings.

BUFFONE: Marinaro was a matinee idol, a Hollywood type. I only got knocked out twice during my career and one of them was in a helmet-to-helmet collision with him. I tackled him. I mean, I really sold out to put a lick on him.

From there, I don't know what the hell happened.

When I got back to the bench, one of our guys came by, patted me on the back and said, "You should see Marinaro. He went back to his huddle screaming, 'I'm hurt, get a timeout.'"

I looked at our guy and said, "Why would I give a shit about Marinaro? Look at me for God's sake."

Our trainer, Freddie Caito, and the medical staff came by and held up some fingers to see if I was "alert." Whenever I got dinged, I'd always put up three fingers. I figured that was probably the best guess I had.

I do remember that I was seeing stars, but really everything was very bright, almost blinding. I was Bernadette at Lourdes. Swear to God.

Hell, it's part of the game—it is the game.

COPPOCK: Why three fingers?

BUFFONE: Because I figured that was my best shot to get back into the game. I thought that made me even money. Half the time I should have put up a middle finger but, shit, I wanted to play. No guy who's worth a damn wants to go into a locker-room after a game having spent half the afternoon on the bench because he got dinged.

In the case of Marinaro, I think I was out two, maybe three plays. What really burned me up was having a lightweight like Marinaro cause me to miss playing time. He was a pretty boy, no more, no less.

COPPOCK: I want to talk about John Brockington, the ex-Ohio State Buckeye. But first, educate the class about "selling out."

BUFFONE: Selling out was "all or nothing" on every play. If you don't "sell out" in the NFL, you're a goner. When you saw guys who began to arm tackle instead of trying to lay the wood, that meant they no longer had the guts to sell out.

To me, selling out was non-negotiable. It was my job. I was an NFL player.

The first time I made contact with a guy, I wanted to win that battle in the worst way. If you have a top-of-the-line running back and he wins the first round, you're probably in for a long afternoon.

When you sell out—and you damn well better do it just as much in the fourth quarter as you do in the first—you're really saying, "I fear nothing.

Come at me with everything you've got because I've got more than you got. I go beyond 100 percent. I'll kick your ass onto the street."

You're trying to make a running back respect your presence because you don't fear even the tiniest thing. Again, if he thinks for one second that you're a wuss, you've given him the mental edge.

You're dead.

COPPOCK: Shrinks call this a "fight-or-flight" reaction. What you're talking about has nothing to do with how much you can bench press. It's all about what you can deal with mentally. This game is ultra-psychological.

BUFFONE: I hear ya. I never backed down from anybody.

Tight ends were the guys I wanted to pound. I didn't care if it was Mackey, Charlie Sanders, or Jackie Smith. I never backed down. You can't play 14 years in this league if you back down. The guys who won't sell out are exposed in this game real fast.

You know when I was in training camp, I could tell in the first two days who was gonna survive the final cut and who was out.

You see how a guy reacts. You just know. Obviously, this game isn't for everybody.

COPPOCK: What you're talking about reminds me of the 24-zip licking the Bears gave the Los Angeles Rams in the NFC title game back on January 12, 1986. The Rams were no match for the Bears. Mike Ditka could have played Stevie Wonder at quarterback and won by 17. The game didn't need to go 60 minutes to determine a winner.

It ended the first time Eric Dickerson carried the ball.

On his first touch, Dickerson didn't hit the line of scrimmage with any kind of authority and he was crushed by Steve McMichael and Mike Singletary.

That goes back to your point.

Dickerson was mamby-pamby tentative while Mongo and Mike were no-holds barred and terrifying. Eric got eaten up from the get-go and was a nonfactor from that moment on. With him neutralized, the Bears easily advanced to the Super Bowl.

BUFFONE: To play pro football, you have to have an on and off switch. You play like a goddamn gladiator for three hours. You may as well be wearing a toga and waving a sword. It may as well be 54 B.C. But when the game ends, you have to pop the off lever. It's not easy.

Tell me the last time a week went by that you didn't hear about some NFL player getting in trouble. You know some guys are just bad people, but I really believe more often than not, that the guys who get in big trouble just don't have the on and off switch.

COPPOCK: I'll make it a point to mention that to Pacman Jones, Sam Hurd, and maybe, Ray Lewis.

chapter 16

Say Amen and Grab a Cigarette

COPPOCK: I honestly can't recall just exactly when groups of NFL players began to have prayer sessions on the field after ballgames. It may have been 1990, when a group of 49ers and Giants kneeled together after a mean-spirited 7–3 ballgame won by the Niners. Now, I do know that in '90 or maybe '91, I was talking to Jim Finks about guys kneeling in prayer. Jim, of course, had gravitated from the Bears to a tenure as president of the Cubs, before venturing way down yonder to the bayou to run the New Orleans Saints. With the Saints, Jim took a gridiron mortuary and made it legitimate. Finks knew talent and he knew how to build from the ground up.

Now, at the time, Jim was trying to convince the NFL to ban postgame prayer. Jim wasn't anti-religion or anti-God by any stretch. Here was his pitch. He felt that after a game, the longer players remained on the field, the more they might be in danger of some nutcase running out from the stands with some kind of weapon or a group of idiots just trying to get TV face time. Actually, I thought Jim's logic made a great deal of sense. Finks believed, as do I, that players have every right to pray in their locker-room.

You know this as well as I do. Booze, football, gambling, and hot tempers don't make for the world's greatest, warm-and-fuzzy postgame sessions. Agreed?

I don't miss the food, but I still miss the bar we had at Sweetwater.

BUFFONE: Yes, let me tell you about God and football, and I believe this sincerely. I'll argue this point with anybody. Do people really think God cares about football? Jeez, we live in a world where hunger, famine, and terrorists are all over the place. Is God supposed to wake up on Sunday and think, "Hey, I really like the Buffalo Bills plus-seven versus the Vikings?" Please. I've always thought God has better things to do with his time. I never went to Sunday mass before a game and prayed to God that we would win. Never—not once.

Listen, this is football, not little kids starving in some third-world country. Some people may think that's a lousy form of sportsmanship. If so, I'm sorry. However, those people are wrong. God doesn't bless the Bears, or for that matter, the Houston Texans.

Ask yourself this question: Why would God pick sides? Do people think God bets the under?

COPPOCK: I see where you're coming from. That reminds me in a roundabout way of Bobby Layne, the legendary Hall of Fame quarterback who played for the Lions and Pittsburgh.

I'd swear Bobby was the last position player to play without a bar or a bird cage on his helmet. Layne was also a notorious drinker. Randy White, the old Dallas Cowboy, gave me a doozey on Bobby. Randy, who shared the MVP Award in Super Bowl 12 (XII, if you must) with Harvey Martin, when the Cowboys clocked Red Miller and the Denver Broncos, was a guy who could party. Years ago, maybe 35 years ago, White was invited by one of Layne's buddies to go on a week-long fishing trip.

Randy, who is just one great guy, said that Layne would begin the day at 6:00 AM with a double martini. Bobby would just guzzle all day. According to Randy, eating with Bobby was strictly optional. Hey, that was just Bobby being Bobby, like Manny being Manny, or Trestman being Trestman.

In the early '60s, Layne wrote in his autobiography *Always on Sunday* that when he'd go to church with his teammates, some guys would pray not to get hurt, but that he always prayed to win.

It was fairly common knowledge around the NFL that Layne used to love to bet on his clubs, so I always wondered if Bobby asked the good lord to give the Lions or Steelers a cover.

But, let's get back to praying and throw in a side dish of handshakes.

BUFFONE: Okay, while you recite the Lord's Prayer, let's talk about handshakes. I just wasn't big on them—period. I know a lot of guys like to say hi to old friends or former college teammates before games. I never got into that. Is that gonna make you play better football? I don't think so, little buddy.

Hey, I only shook hands before the coin toss because I had to do it.

This may sound painfully old school to some people, but I never, ever helped a guy get off the ground.

Why would I? I didn't expect the son of a bitch on the other side of the ball to help me up. If we saw each other in a social environment, that was a whole different thing. Then I'd be cordial as hell. As for postgames, I didn't have any interest in long goodbyes. I didn't want to stick around and ask a guy how his wife and kids are doing, or about the boating trip he was planning for the off-season.

In other words, I wasn't big on Kumbayaing.

COPPOCK: Timeout. Did you say Kumbayaing? I don't think we're gonna find that word in Webster's or the *National Enquirer.*

BUFFONE: (Laughing) I hear ya. But I didn't do any Kumbayaing after a ballgame. I was really too wrapped up in what I had done or hadn't done.

Coppock, I told you years ago that when you played on lousy ballclubs—and I played on far too many of them—you survive by judging your own performance. It keeps you from going overboard mentally.

Again, I can hear people saying I wasn't displaying sportsmanship. No, that isn't it. It was my mindset. Was there some NFL rule that after a game, I had to tell half the guys on the Philadelphia Eagles that I loved them? Plus, let's mention the obvious: I was anxious to get in the locker-room and have a cigarette.

COPPOCK: I have to believe that Butkus also had an influence on you, right?

BUFFONE: Oh, hell yes. You talk to Dick about sportsmanship and he'll tell you, "Sportsmanship, my ass." I felt the same way. We both played the game as if it was a fight where the last guy standing was the winner.

That reminds me of "Hang," a play we used to run with O.B. all the time. Now, keep in mind, you obviously couldn't get away with this in today's NFL. Hang was O.B. extending his arm in parallel fashion. His real intent wasn't to tackle a ball carrier. He was just trying to lay out the guy. He could clothesline because he knew we'd have a guy filling the gap to make a stop.

It was like going across the middle with wideouts. I'm actually glad rules have changed to protect receivers. People just have no clue how helpless receivers are running a crossing route, or for that matter a seam. They're really helpless. A guy having a free shot to blast the guy into the middle of next week just flies in the face of what the game is really all about.

Do you remember a wideout we had named Dick Gordon?

COPPOCK: Damn right. The guy was superb. Plus, he may have been the greatest fashion plate in NFL history. I remember Gordon and Halas were always butting heads about money. Finally, after '71, when free agency was still in its infancy—the players basically had no rights—Gordon signed with the Rams. The Bears got a first-round pick, but had to wait two years to use the choice.

Muggs Halas went nuts with anger. He damn near tore (then-NFL Commissioner) Pete Rozelle's head off in the press. Rozelle had essentially orchestrated the deal by declaring that any club that signed Gordon would have to give up a first rounder two seasons down the road. Team Halas—Muggs and the Old Man—thought they had worked out a legitimate trade with the Rams. Really, they had every right to be ticked off.

You're going to tell me Gordon wasn't special? He led the NFL in receiving in 1970 with 71 catches and 13 TDs, with Bobby Douglass and Jack Concannon at quarterback. In other words, he didn't have Joe Montana or John Elway pitching. That was '71, when most team were still going with just two wideouts and the league was still a haven for running backs. Dick went to the Pro Bowl in both '70 and '71.

BUFFONE: If Dick played with today's rules, he'd catch 115 balls a year.

COPPOCK: Dick used to live at clothing stores up and down Wells Street. One of the joints he loved was called The Man at Ease. The guy just dressed to kill. I recall one night when he showed up for taping, he was wearing boots up to his knees and a full-length, silver fox fur coat. The guy was a character, but the guy could flat-out play. Duffy Daugherty, his coach at Michigan State, was crazy about Dick.

chapter 17

Can't Win for Losin'

COPPOCK: Hey, gang, have I mentioned yet that losing, you know, can be a bitch?

You need to adopt that thought as we continue our journey through the life and times of Doug Buffone.

Here's your primer, a handful of games in which the Bears played so pathetically awful that you would've sworn guys were wearing thumbtacks instead of football cleats and shoulder pads made out of shag carpeting.

Example: The worst double-dip, single-season nightmare versus their most hated ancient rival? In 1962, Lombardi and the Pack walloped the Bears 49–0 up north. However, the Bears did show dramatic improvement when the two clubs met in a rematch later that year at Cubs Park.

They lost to Green Bay 38–7. I'd swear that game was actually tied 7–7 before the Pack decided to bring out its A-game.

BUFFONE: Oh, please!

COPPOCK: Here's another one. Worst indoor loss in a temperature controlled environment? The 1977 Bears lost to the Houston Oilers in the Astrodome 47–0.

Remarkably, that Bears team somehow made the playoffs for the first time in 14 years.

Most miserable swan dive at home in the postseason in so-called, "Bear Weather?" Ditka and friends were blown out of Soldier Field by Joe Montana and the 49ers in the 1988 NFC title game 28–3. If common sense had prevailed, the Little League slaughter rule would have been invoked at halftime. The wind chill at game time was 2 degrees above zero. The wind chill was nuts. It had to be 30-below in the lakefront mausoleum. Fortunately, the Honey Bears had been retired by Virginia McCaskey three years earlier. The poor babes would have collapsed from frostbite—or maybe from the boredom of the Bears offense.

Hey, Buffone, feel free to join the party. Let's talk about 1969, a year that tested the mettle of anybody who held cherished Bears season tickets. It was the worst year in the storied history of the franchise.

BUFFONE: People think they know how tough losing is, but they really don't. Think about the crap we went through in 1969. I don't know if we drank more booze, but we sure as hell didn't drink any less.

We were outta the damn race by the third week. Jim Dooley was our coach and people ask me, "Did Dooley ever get any advice from Halas about how he was coaching the team?"

And, knowing Dooley, I tell 'em George probably said, "Avoid the race track."

COPPOCK: I remember Dooley was ragged about what Ed Stone from the old *Chicago Today* was writing about the club.

So what did he do?

Jim, a guy I really liked, banned Stoney from the dressing room. Ed told me he had to interview Butkus outdoors in November in 25-degree weather.

BUFFONE: I don't accept excuses and the problem in '69 was that we had guys who did lie down. They took the easy way out. They just played for the paycheck.

But I also know this: Our fans knew the guys who were putting out, playing hard, and they were behind us.

You think Butkus would lie down?

Christ, he got madder as the weeks went along.

You know, after the way we finished '68, with a club that really should have won the division, we thought '69 was gonna be special. You know, our year.

I've never forgotten just how rotten that season was and I never will.

COPPOCK: Let me fill in some blanks. The '69 Bears, unquestionably the most embarrassing team in franchise history, went a lugubrious 1–13. The atmosphere was so poisonous that late in the year, Virgil Carter, a halfway decent quarterback from Brigham Young, was suspended by the Old Man for calling the Bears a "chicken-shit organization."

Would you like a world-class chunk of irony?

Two years later as a member of the Cincinnati Bengals, Carter led the NFL in passing.

But that's just the prelim.

By the late '70s, Virgil was back with the Bears via a trade with San Diego. He also did some broadcast work with the club. I'm still stunned that the Old Man let him within 200 miles of Chicago.

BUFFONE: What Carter did took a lot of guts. He really spoke for a lot of people. But, who in the hell was Virgil Carter?

He was a backup. He was a nobody.

His comments obviously didn't mean anything to the ballclub. Jesus, it was still another four to five years before Jim Finks got to town.

COPPOCK: I remember seeing Carter at O'Hare Field on the Friday after he made the legendary "chicken-shit" remarks. He was a lot of things, but he wasn't apologetic. He told me, "Somebody had to say what I did. So, I'm actually glad I did say what needed to be said." I thought Halas would tell his fellow NFL club owners to blackball the guy.

BUFFONE: Think about that season. We were the most valiant losers since, well...the guys defending the Alamo. They had a lousy year, too.

The first question I always ask myself is how a club with Dick Butkus and Gale Sayers lost 13 games—and, some people don't know that we only played 14 in those days.

Sayers was tremendous. Here's a guy who had knee surgery in 1968 after he was drilled by the 49ers' Kermit Alexander at Wrigley Field. I can still feel the deadly silence in the ball park as Gale was carried off the field. If Sayers played today, he would have come back just fine, but doctors didn't know then what they know now. Not by a long shot.

Gale had to work his ass off to get ready to play in '69. But he wasn't the same Sayers. He just couldn't run outside. He couldn't cut. What he did do was play on guts, running behind an o-line that was mediocre on its good days.

The guy became a straight-ahead runner and he went on to lead the league in rushing (1,032 yards, longest carry 28 yards). I remember Dooley benched him about the fourth or fifth week up at Detroit.

How the hell do you bench Gale Sayers?

Hell, we celebrated if we won the coin toss.

COPPOCK: Buff, two things come to mind when I think about the "Comet" in '69. One, the Bears called a press conference for Gale some time in early July. The club's stance, or thought process, was that it would give Gale a chance to talk about his recovery from surgery so that he wouldn't be badgered by the press once training camp opened.

You saw a new and more polished Gale Sayers. He answered every query about his knee and his subsequent rehab. He fielded questions for about 30 minutes. He couldn't have been more candid. He was remarkably succinct... not at all like the rookie who joined the Bears in '65. That Sayers had to be pinned to a wall to say four words. He was just a terribly shy country kid.

So, game over, right?

No.

Channel 5's diminutive Johnny Erp grabbed Sayers for a "separate" after the conference and the first question out of his mouth was, "Gale, I wanna ask you again, just how's that knee?"

Dana and I holding court with longtime friend and Hall of Famer Joe Namath.

Sayers looked at Johnny like he was an escapee from a downstate mental ward.

Secondly, the Bears opened the preseason in D.C. versus Washington. It was Lombardi's first game as head coach of the 'Skins.

A downpour hit the ballpark about half an hour before kickoff. The field was a quagmire. So what does Sayers do?

He takes the opening kickoff back about 70 yards.

I was there. I spotted the game for Lloyd Pettit and Irv Kupcinet and producer Jack Rosenberg for WGN Radio. I had to ask myself, "What the hell is a precious commodity like Gale Sayers doing returning kicks in the first of six preseason games?"

BUFFONE: That just tells you where the whole organization was at that time. It was pathetic. The players weren't stupid. We were just bewildered by how things were operating.

I remember seeing our personnel guy, Bobby Walston, around that time. I said to myself after we talked, "This guy's clueless."

Do you remember that game we lost at St. Louis?

That would tell you all you needed to know about how crummy '69 was. We're on the road and our quarterback, Jack Concannon, decided to call a timeout at the line of scrimmage, but our center didn't understand what Jack said, so he figured it was "hut" and snapped the ball.

Anyway, the damn ball goes flying in the air and it's caught by one of the Cardinals (Larry Stallings) and the lucky bastard walked into the end zone.

Naturally, we go on to lose.

Again.

COPPOCK: I don't know how you kept yourself in check. From 1969 to 1975, the Bears went 28–69–1. They weren't just bad; they were an NFL disgrace.

I hate to rap the Old Man and his son, Muggs, but son of a bitch, they didn't know which way was up—or down for that reason. I'd like to know how many good football players the Old Man and Muggsy didn't contact because they dared to have agents. I revered the Old Man as I know you did, and Muggs was really a terrific guy, but the NFL had left them confused. They just didn't recognize the radical changes the league was undergoing, economically, socially, and for that reason, racially. You know the Bears were the last team in the NFL to send out press releases. Go figure. Ed Stone used to joke that Muggs was so secretive that, "If he had it his way, he would order the Bears not to release their schedule."

BUFFONE: This might sound crazy, but here's how I managed to get by. I knew I had the respect of my peers. I'd heard through the grapevine that Dallas and the Steelers were both interested in picking me up.

I'll tell you one thing: that really meant a lot to me.

Andy Russell (Pittsburgh linebacker, seven time Pro Bowl selection) told me he learned off my technique. Think about that. Russell was playing with guys like Jack Lambert and Jack Ham, and he told me that he perfected his style of play from watching me.

Maybe, I should have asked the Bears to trade me back in the early '70s, but I always told myself that Chicago would be the perfect place to be if we could just win.

God, I was in the game for 12 years before I finally went to the playoffs.

There's only one thing teams couldn't do back in those days; they couldn't outfight us. You can take that to the bank, Jack.

I remember that during the '69 season, I became really ill. I honest to gosh think it was because of the anxiety I felt. The losing just kills you. Sports are different than real life. The games are so damn big. The losses eat at you. It's not a 9-to-5 job at the local 7-Eleven.

You know what's odd about all of this? After my last year in '79, Finks wanted me to stay with the ballclub. He offered me a new two-year deal at over $150,000 a year.

I told him, "Jim, I just don't have anything left and I sure as hell don't want to embarrass myself." Finks told me I could teach the young kids and be a part-time player.

No dice. It was time.

I'm glad I walked away.

That was really a new era for me. I separated from my first wife, Linda, in '79 and then we divorced in '81. I married Dana, the best thing that ever happened to me. I really mean that. Dana has been beyond a blessing.

I've always said that football player shouldn't get married young. There are too many distractions, if you know what I mean. They should wait until they're about 35 and have pro football out of their system.

COPPOCK: There is something to be said about focus.

BUFFONE: No shit.

chapter 18

When You Gotta Go, You Gotta GO!

COPPOCK: Now, the defense will prove that on April 15, 2000, Doug Buffone illustrated remarkable clairvoyance regarding the NFL draft and displayed brilliant spontaneity that same afternoon as he attended to "the Call of Nature."

Additionally, the defense will also prove beyond a shadow of a doubt that, very simply, it is understandable that "under dire physiological circumstances, a man does what he has to do."

I ask the jury to please heed the following exhibits:

Exhibit A: rest stop on the toll road somewhere in Illinois.

Exhibit B: a careening automobile skidding chaotically into the parking lot.

Exhibit C: a muscular Italian man running like a jewel thief into the restroom.

I ask the defendant, tell your story to the jury, sir.

BUFFONE: I had an appearance to make in Orland Park, way the hell south of Lake Forest. So after the Bears made the Urlacher draft pick (Round 1, 9th overall) late in the afternoon, I ran out to my car and jumped on the toll road.

COPPOCK: (To the jury) This is just the rising action; get ready for my client's knockout punch.

BUFFONE: Suddenly, I've got the green-apple quick step. I mean, my bowels are just dying to get to a bathroom, any bathroom. So, I land at one of those rest stops you find on the toll roads and I see a sign by a washroom that says, "Closed for construction."

So, I rush in the other door not entirely paying attention to where the hell I'm going since all I cared about was "going," if you catch my drift. I thought I was in a men's room, but at that point, beggars can't be choosers, right?

Suddenly I notice, there are no urinals. So, I sat down in a stall and I'm smoking a cigar and, you know, doing my business, which is a very polite austere way of saying I was taking a...well, you know.

COPPOCK: Let the record state, an All-Pro crap.

BUFFONE: Yeah. Everything seemed okay when outta nowhere, a bunch of women come into the washroom. I mean, not two or three, but a busload of ladies.

So, what the hell do I do? I'm a public figure. I'm a Chicago Bear for Christ's sake.

I'm in a ladies room and smoking a cigar.

Now, I know nobody's gonna believe this, but it's a fact. One of the ladies begins sniffling around and asks, "Is that a *cigar?*" So, I ditch the stogie. Meanwhile, I pulled my feet up since I'm obviously wearing shoes.

COPPOCK: Men's shoes.

BUFFONE: Hell yeah, men's shoes!

COPPOCK: Bruno Maglis?

BUFFONE: Wingtips. I swear, my heart had to be running at a hundred beats a minute. God, I was dying in there.

Then, one of these babes knocks on my stall door and impatiently asks, "Are you almost done?"

What in the hell do I say now?

So, I threw my voice as high as I could and chirped, "Almost, honey!"

COPPOCK: (Dramatically gesturing to the jury on Doug's behalf) Wait a second, you don't have a voice like Barry White, but I can't see you tossing up a falsetto that's gonna make people forget about Frankie Valli or Celine Dion.

BUFFONE: Well, somehow the gals bought it. Of course, they could have been drunk.

COPPOCK: Let the record further show that the defendant astutely deceived a roomful of aggressive women to save his, uh...

BUFFONE: Ass.

COPPOCK: You got that right.

BUFFONE: I had women going to the bathroom on both sides of me. I swear to ya, I was sweating bullets. I imagined 25 women busting the door down and one of them screaming, "My God, it's DOUG BUFFONE...and he's... shitting!"

I told God, "If you can get me out of this one, I swear I will never cuss on the field again."

COPPOCK: Let the jury note that Buffone just cursed.

BUFFONE: Who are you...Perry Mason or Father Flanagan?

COPPOCK: Just the facts!

BUFFONE: Finally, after about 10 minutes, they left.

Now, what the hell would I have done if one of those girls had seen me and called security? You know I would have been busted.

COPPOCK: My first reaction is whoever booked you would have recognized you and at least asked for your autograph.

Jeez, I can just see Ron Magers busting his jugular vein on the Channel 7 News while screaming that, "A legendary Chicago Bear linebacker is in trouble with the law tonight."

The story would have left, shall we say, a lengthy paper trail.

Pun intended.

BUFFONE: Just suppose I'd been caught? Can you imagine what the hell would have happened? I mean, suppose if one of those ladies had called the cops. I would have been fired. I mean waxed from everything. I would have had to leave town for Christ's sake.

COPPOCK: Look on the bright side. You would have been a front-page story in both the downtown dailies along with the *Herald*, and you would have topped the 10 o'clock news for at least two nights.

Who could ask for anything more?

Frankly, this was just too funny.

BUFFONE: Yeah, great. Anyway, I had said for at least a week that the Bears would take Urlacher in the first round. Greg Blache, the Bears D-coordinator, kept on saying he was going to be a strong side 'backer. I never bought it. I said the kid would play the middle. He was so darn athletic that he had to play the middle.

You know Brian was a safety at New Mexico, so he already knew all about dropping into coverage.

COPPOCK: I was with Skip Bayless—the former *Trib* columnist, now with ESPN—up at Halas Hall. He shared your theory. He thought Urlacher was going to be a Mike.

But Skip had to fight to get his thoughts into the paper. Some guy on the desk at the *Tribune* called Bayless and told him he couldn't write that Urlacher was going to play the middle because Blache said he was gonna play the strong side.

Now, Skip is a standup guy, and he'll fight like hell for anything he believes in. So he tells his co-workers, "I don't care what the hell Blache says or what the Bears say—this guy is gonna play the Mike."

BUFFONE: And of course, he did. Very well, too.

COPPOCK: In conclusion, do you have any advice for guys with the green-apple quick step?

BUFFONE: Yes. Wait until you find a Denny's, or maybe a Popeye's...they have more stalls.

COPPOCK: Ladies and gentleman of the jury, you have no alternative but to render a verdict of "Not guilty" in the case of "Doug Buffone in the Inhospitable Hen House."

chapter 19

Buffone Answers All Mail

COPPOCK: Doug, we've known each other since Richard Nixon was running the show, so I really doubt this will come as any surprise to you. My mind's been wandering. I've been giving a lot of thought to Marshawn Lynch and his refusal to speak to the press. Have you got that?

BUFFONE: Carry on.

COPPOCK: It just made me think about how much I've seen go down with the NFL over the past 50-plus years.

Think about the size and scope of that frolic known as Super Bowl media day. Every lunatic this side of Chris Berman shows up to ask Tom Brady if he wears boxers or briefs or, maybe, some wild-eyed kid from a morning zoo radio show will take on Russell Wilson by asking him, "If you were a tree, what kind of tree would you want to be?" You know I'm kidding, but not by much.

Think about how Super Bowl media days bumped the stock of MTV Jock "Downtown" Julie Brown. She became a press day legend. She damn near got interviewed as much time as big-name players. As a rule, 10 days before the Super Bowl, there really isn't much to say about the game. Am I supposed to furiously grab a paper with a headline that reads, "Favre Fears New England Defense" or "Parcells Says Turnovers Will Be the difference"?

The NFL Network generally starts running "Noted special teams tackles from the 1960s" by the Tuesday before the big game actually takes place.

Let me tell you a quick story that shouldn't last more than 15 minutes. Now, imagine this. Way back in 1962, the Bears drafted Ronnie Bull, a hard-nosed running back out of Baylor. Ronnie could flat out play. No, he wasn't Gale Sayers, but he was a *Sports Illustrated* cover boy his first year with Coach Halas. Plus "The Bull" was chosen NFL Rookie of the Year. The Old Man kept on feeding Ronnie the ball in the fourth quarter to burn clock time when the Bears knocked off Allie Sherman and the Giants 14–10 to win the Old Man's last NFL title back in '63. Bull was a north-south, bread-and-butter running back who never hesitated to challenge a linebacker. He played Texas tough.

Now, follow me on this. A little while after Ronnie was drafted, Halas brought him to Chicago to see the Bears play the Detroit Lions. If you're scoring at home, in arctic-like conditions, the Bears white-washed the Lions 3–0. Doug Atkins must have had four sacks.

But I digress. Papa Bear decided to have Ronnie sit in the legendary "auxiliary" press box. My old man, Charles Coppock, who just loved the Bears like crazy, was very tight with the Old Man, so we were also sitting in that box—right next to Ronnie.

Halfway through the first quarter, you could tell that Bull was freezing to death. The poor guy had his traditional crew cut with no hat and he was wearing a very light overcoat. It had to be about 12 degrees outside with the wind blowing out of the east right into our kissers.

Now, people are gonna call me a liar when I tell you this but, honest to God, it's on the square. Luke Johnsos, Halas' longtime assistant coach and offensive eye in the sky, popped out of his booth that was adjacent to where Bull and I were sitting and handed me a note.

On a very small piece of scrap paper, the guy I called Uncle Luke wrote a message to Ed Rozy, the team's trainer, telling him to give me one of the club's warm-up jackets, so Ronnie could avoid hypothermia. Think about that. I'm 14 years old, and with the game in progress, Luke has me go down to see Ed Rozy to get a warm-up jacket.

Where was security? I never saw any. I got down to the front row behind the old Bears bench at midfield on the third-base side of Wrigley Field and asked Mr. Rozy to step over. I showed him the note and he asked, "Are you

Charlie's kid?" I said yes and Ed gave me two warm-up jackets with a warning that if I lost them or some drunk stole them, I'd pay with my ass.

Really, can you make this stuff up?

It made me think about how much the league has grown over the years. It also makes me wonder how much money you would have made if you played in the so-called modern era. When you played, gas was 29 cents per gallon and I'd bet 99 percent of the home TVs in Chicago were black and white. Lyndon Johnson was in office. Martin Luther King had become an iconic figure.

Doug Buffone & Norm Van Lier
"The Bear & The Bull"

God took him much too soon. I loved tag-teaming with Norm Van Lier on radio.

BUFFONE: You know, it's interesting. I do wonder from time to time just how big my name would be if I had all the exposure that guys have today. You know in my later years, I had the "Doug Buffone Report," but we didn't have anywhere near the coverage guys get today. Guess what? We didn't know what a dot.com was and we were, what, 35 years away from email?

COPPOCK: That stack of mail you're holding has got to tell you something.

BUFFONE: I still get about 10 or 15 letters a week from fans asking me to sign a picture or just give them my autograph on a piece of paper. Look at this, I've got mail here from New Jersey, Wisconsin, Minnesota, and Pennsylvania. I get some letters from people in Chicago, but really, the bulk of what I get comes from out of state.

You know how most of the letters read? They'll say, "I never saw you play, but my father told me that you were a terrific football player." I find that very flattering. I haven't played for almost four decades, but there are clearly people out there who remember what I brought to the game. It means a lot.

COPPOCK: Do you ever worry that the autograph hounds are just memorabilia hustlers who want to take your, shall we say, "personal equity" and sell it on eBay or at a card show?

BUFFONE: Hell, no. I've never given it any thought at all. What the hell, if some guy can make a few bucks off of me, go ahead and do it. (Laughter) Maybe, you're on to something. I know, I'll establish the "Buffone College Fund" to help out Dana and me with the college tuition we're going to have for our twin girls. I told you before, Coppock, the last check I write before they put me under ground will be a tuition check.

COPPOCK: Pssst. Doug does not email. I have to believe that he thinks "Facebook" might be a restaurant in San Francisco or a shot-and-beer joint in Houston. I am hardly a computer genius, but every time I sit down with Buff, I feel like maybe I was the guy who invented the Internet. I keep telling Doug he should hop on to YouTube just to see himself in action or click on Google images to see what he looked like when his 235 pounds body was a massive chunk of bone and steel-tough muscle.

BUFFONE: I can't hide this, but I love when my kids tell me they see me in a Bears uniform. Any father wants his kids to be proud of him and I'm proud as hell when one of my twins tells me she saw me on some computer thing. Maybe, in my next life, I'll learn email, but I doubt it.

COPPOCK: Doug looked noticeably thin as we gathered for this round of give and take. The fact is he had several medical issues to deal with over the past years or so. One problem required a form of irrigation.

Doug told me the medics told him his body was simply retaining too much water. Doug said removing the excess fluid from his system dropped his weight about 25 pounds. However, his outlook on life remained rosy, very positive.

He was also coping with a sore knee. Then again, tell me any 70-year-old football player who isn't dealing with at least nine different sets of aches and pains. It is what it is—and what it was. It's why I don't pass judgment on what football players are earning today. They risk life and limb every time they lace on cleats.

chapter 20

K.C. and the Slaughterhouse Band

COPPOCK: You have to have some mileage on the tires to remember the gridiron debacle way back in 1967, maybe 80,000 miles worth. If so, your radials weren't the only things with treads wearing thin on that evening.

Remarkably, a defeat of this magnitude has been spit out by the history books. It's almost as if it never happened. This right uppercut was, after all, absorbed 47 years ago in what was George Halas' final season as head coach of the "the Monsters of the Midway." The Bears, like any other team, have played some games that were so excruciating, so downright hapless and hopeless, that you don't bother to look at the tape.

You burn it.

Or, on second thought, maybe you have your roster face a firing squad or demand they watch soccer 12 hours a day for two weeks.

For openers, knowing how much Halas was an insufferable loser, I'm convinced he really never got over this ass-kicking. The Old Man just hated losing. The losses just ripped at his very fabric.

His beloved Bears, the cornerstone franchise upon which the NFL was built, weren't just trounced, they were battered into submission by the Kansas City Chiefs of the American Football League, 66–24.

Payback is great motivation in sports history. In 1916, Georgia Tech exacted revenge on Cumberland College for a loss in baseball in 1915. The final score of their next football game was 222–0. No, Tech was not a 221-point favorite.

You can look it up.

Now, comes the team sacked by the mighty NFL the previous January in their first Super Bowl.

It wasn't pretty.

On August 23, 1967, the Bears went fumbling into the old 33,000-seat phone booth known as Memorial Stadium in Kansas City to face the Chiefs from the so-called "minor league," the AFL.

Listen, the Chiefs knew all about the big boys.

Seven months earlier, they had faced Vince Lombardi in the first AFL-NFL title game at the Los Angeles Coliseum. The Chiefs got licked by the Green Bay machine, but I do recall that K.C. more than held its own.

In fact, the Chiefs outgained Bart Starr and the Pack and were in the hunt, trailing just 14–10 at the half.

Seeing how easily their NFL brethren, the Packers, dominated K.C. in the second half, the Bears strolled into the game half-heartedly and with all the buzz of warm beer.

To quote Vivian as she smirked at the Rodeo Drive sales snob in *Pretty Woman*.

Big mistake. Big.

Huge.

BUFFONE: We set ourselves up to get hammered. The thought with our guys was, hey, this was just the AFL. We were crazy enough to think that we were the better team. We walked in without a worry in the world.

I don't know what the hell we were thinking. They made us look terrible. If it was a TV ratings war, they were *Gunsmoke* and we were *F-Troop.*

My God. We just got clobbered. We were pathetic.

Hank Stram and the Chiefs were loaded. Do you remember who they had on defense?

Christ, Buck Buchanan was a monster. So were Willie Lanier, E.J. Holub, and Bobby Bell. Plus, they had the "Big Cat" Ernie Ladd, who also made a lot of money as a professional wrestler. The guy was a terrific "heel" or villain, whatever they call those guys.

We were ant hills and they were the Alps.

Len Dawson, a Hall of Famer, was their quarterback. They were loaded with guys who could make big plays. Think Otis Taylor and Mike Garrett, for openers.

We just weren't ready to play.

COPPOCK: Brace yourself…the Mini Cooper meets the Mack truck. The Chiefs led the Bears 39–10 at halftime on the way to a 66–24 victory—66 dominating points.

No Bears team, before or since, working an exhibition or regular season game, has ever given up that many points in one ballgame. Good God, this game got so badly out of hand that K.C. put up 32 points on the Bears in the second quarter.

BUFFONE: You know what I remember most about that mess? The Chiefs had a horse and every time they'd score, that damn animal would circle the stadium. The horse ran himself to death. I can still see him lying down in the fourth quarter.

I almost prayed that he would have a heart attack like that stallion did in *Animal House.*

Bobby Joe Green, our punter, made me laugh late in the game. After we actually came up with a stop, Bobby grabbed me near the sidelines and said, "Let's get outta here. They might wanna keep on playing."

Halas was angry as hell, and I don't blame the Old Man. Some guys have said that Halas actually began crying out of anger at halftime.

At that time, Halas was still the most powerful owner in the NFL. The only guy who had equal authority with Halas was Pete Rozelle. And I'm not really sure if Pete had as much influence over the league as Halas did.

COPPOCK: Several guys have told me Halas just wept his eyes out at halftime. He wasn't crying because of Kansas City. Halas had to feel emasculated. His beloved club had just let down the entire National Football League.

Look at that follow-through! I won the Bears home run derby at old Comiskey Park in the late '70s.

BUFFONE: Halas got a bad break. We had to go back on the field. You know during the pregame warm-ups we came out in our jerseys and shoulder pads. The Chiefs came out in T-shirts. They just looked huge…biggest team I'd ever seen. I turned to Butkus and said, "Dick, this isn't gonna be pretty." After the game, Halas just burned the game film, or so I'm told. I know as players we never saw the damn thing.

COPPOCK: Cooper Rollow, a gentleman's gentleman who later became sports editor of the *Tribune*, covered the blowout for the *Trib*. He wrote: "With Mike Garrett and Curtis McClinton running like stallions, the Chiefs pulverized the right side of the Bear defense, where [Marty] Amsler was perspiring in futile agony, as they marched 72 yards in 13 plays."

You know, Amsler was a nice guy. He just wasn't any threat to the legacy of Doug Atkins.

BUFFONE: Well said. Really, the guy just didn't have the goods to play. I don't know how he made our club. Maybe, it tells you how little talent we really had.

You know I've had one thought about that for years.

This game meant the world to Kansas City. They had been knocked off in the first Super Bowl, or whatever the hell they called it, and afterward Lombardi said that the Chiefs just weren't as good as some of the clubs in the NFL.

I don't know exactly what Vince said, but I know it had to sting Kansas City.

COPPOCK: Lombardi, verbatim: "I don't think they're as good as the top teams in the National Football League. They're a good team with fine speed, but I'd have to say the NFL is tougher."

BUFFONE: Did Lombardi say something else?

COPPOCK: Yeah, get ready for the dagger. Now, mind you, Lombardi was under enormous pressure to win this game. And not just from the fans in

Titletown, but also from Halas, Wellington Mara, and Arthur Rooney, guys who were the core of the NFL's old guard.

They were scared to death that the NFL might actually get licked.

So, Lombardi, in what I always thought was a major cleansing breath, said, "Dallas is a better club and so are several others. There, you've wanted me to say [it] and I said it."

Hey, Lombardi had a right to thrust his chest out. His guys had just beaten the team from the upstart league by 25 points and recorded six sacks.

He could have been forgiven if he'd said the Chiefs weren't in the NFL's league.

BUFFONE: Let me tell you something. The atmosphere back in Rensselaer after that game was like a funeral. The tension level was miserable. Halas, the coaching staff, and the players were uptight as hell.

We deserved to be embarrassed by the Chiefs and we were. Let me also add this: fuckin' Hank Stram ran the score up on us.

COPPOCK: Hey, this is just too obvious. You guys thought it was going to be a 60-minute vacation against a lesser light, but the lesser light that night was treating the evening like it was the seventh game of the World Series.

This was payback time for them.

I met Ernie Ladd about three years later when he was in town for a wrestling card I helped promote with Bob Luce at old Comiskey Park. The Big Cat told me, "We were sky-high waiting to whip those big, bad Bears. We knew we were gonna kick their ass. We had better guys on the bench than the Bears had on the field."

BUFFONE: Fred Arbanas, the K.C. tight end, always called it their mini-Super Bowl.

COPPOCK: You guys got off easy, Doug. If this game happened in today's Twitter, dot.com, internet universe, you would have become a running joke on Letterman, Fallon, and Kimmel for weeks.

It was the Old Man's final season at the helm. You guys went 7–6–1 during the regular season.

The following year, owner George Halas was up in the press box. I know, I sat right behind him during the games. No kidding.

BUFFONE: No doubt. He was still trying to forget that damn loss to the Chiefs.

COPPOCK: I doubt he ever did.

BUFFONE: I sure as hell won't.

chapter 21

Meet Private Buffone

COPPOCK: How do I describe Frank Cornish without comparing him to a mountainous mass of unrealized potential?

The correct answer is, I don't.

When I think about Cornish, the former defensive tackle with the Bears, two things come immediately to mind. He never came close to truly understanding his God-given ability.

Realizing potential?

He never grasped the concept.

Two, his ever-present girth always looked like it was trying its best to win a 15-round fight with every cheeseburger in the city.

On a good day, Cornish's pronounced gut would generously hang about two inches over his uniform pants. Frank would never be confused with Walter Payton. Hell, he would never be confused with the land mass of Asia.

Sweetness used to run miles up a hill. Cornish balked at the incline of a sand bar. This guy was so big that if he ever went swimming, Ahab would have set him up with his harpoon. This guy was the perfect poster child for triple-thick burritos.

Back in 1968, Jim Dooley, in his first year as head coach of the Bears, decided he was going to make a statement. Maybe, Jim figured that since he had been tapped to replace the venerable George Halas that he had to show his troops that while the Old Man was gone, the Bears would still be run as the proverbial tight ship.

Unfortunately, Cornish, who played for the club from 1965 through 1969, was beyond obese. Dooley's new edict doomed him.

Frank reminded me of a smaller version of the legendary wrestler, Haystacks Calhoun. Calhoun's weight was generally listed at 601 pounds, although having spent an evening downing scotch with 'Stacks in Milwaukee way back in 1971, I'd swear he didn't weigh a dime over 548.

Doug, you of all people, should know that Cornish, your ex-teammate, had bona fide football talent.

BUFFONE: I know what you're talking about. Frank had phenomenal speed for a guy that size. But you just knew his heart really wasn't in the game. He had the goods to be an All-Pro; I mean an out-and-out star.

He could have been a very special talent, but again, he just didn't care enough about the game, or maybe he just thought he could skate through other clubs by using his weight.

COPPOCK: Back to Dooley. Jim decided before one exhibition game to leave Cornish back in Rensselaer. Frank wasn't just on the fat man's table; he was the fat man's table.

Now, here's the subtle twist.

A Chicago sportswriter, I want to say it was Bill Gleason from the *Sun-Times,* went down to spend an evening with Frank as he watched the ballgame. Bill got more than he bargained for with Mr. Cornish.

Here's this athlete who had to weigh 340 pounds, telling Gleason that he really wasn't on a diet; he was just, "cutting down a little." Then, he proceeded to eat a large pizza by himself while his teammates sweated out a football game on TV.

I would have killed to see the expression on Gleason's face.

BUFFONE: Okay, let me tell you a story about Frank Cornish and Doug Buffone that I guarantee you nobody has ever heard.

In 1966, Vietnam was beginning to escalate. It was getting bigger and bigger, and Halas knew there was a good chance that guys like Frank and me could get drafted into the army.

To be honest, I think the Pentagon was better off without me.

So one day, the Old Man calls me in and says, “Listen, you’re going to join the National Guard. But to get this done, you’ve got to go down to Fort Campbell, Kentucky, and go through basic training.”

COPPOCK: I’ve already got this one figured out. No runs, no hits, no conspiracy theory. The Old Man used his clout, made one phone call, and got you and Cornish in the Guard so that he wouldn’t lose you to a full-term hitch in the military.

BUFFONE: Bingo. I wasn’t crazy about going to Fort Campbell, but I did what I had to do.

Let me explain what made basic so damn tough. The new recruits didn’t work by themselves. We were thrust in with the “Screaming Eagles,” the elite paratroopers. These guys were trained bad-asses, just tough as all hell.

These bastards didn’t like us. They did everything in their power to make our lives miserable.

But you know, in a crazy way, I sort of understood what was going on with them. A lot of these guys had already been to ’Nam and they knew they were going back while we were gonna go home.

Can you understand why they thought we were jerks? They’d already seen body bags. They figured we were going back to country clubs.

COPPOCK: How did Cornish survive? The boot camp had to kill the poor son of a gun.

BUFFONE: We took the bus with a bunch of guys down to Fort Campbell. When we arrived, we were met by a sergeant who looked at us all like we were just pieces of shit.

Finally, he said, “I hear we got a couple of guys here from Chicago, that big tough mob town up north. Is that true?” Both Frank and I raised our hands. Now the guy asks, “Have you got any guns on you?”

So, what the hell happened next?

Frank calmly took out a .38 and put it on the table. All of a sudden, our sergeant looked a little edgy. He's not squeamish, but he's a little taken aback. So, he said to Big Frank, "Is that damn thing loaded?"

Cornish looked him right in the eye and said, "Why the hell would I carry it if it wasn't loaded?"

COPPOCK: Why didn't they bust him for carrying a concealed weapon?

BUFFONE: To be honest with you, I think they were afraid of Cornish. Back in 1965 when people thought about Chicago, they thought about Al Capone for Christ's sake.

Watching Frank go through basic was just a riot. First off, it took about a week for them to find a pair of pants that could fit the big guy.

But that's not all. When we're out on maneuvers, Frank was always about three miles behind the pack, but our D.I.s never said a word to him. I think they were afraid he'd step on them. You know, when I got done with Fort Campbell, I was in the greatest shape of my life. I mean, I was a goddamn razor blade.

I think Frank, on the other hand, gained about 30 pounds.

COPPOCK: Are we talking about Doug Buffone for the Purple Heart here?

BUFFONE: Not a chance. But I did go through an experience that was a genuine eye opener.

This bad-ass sergeant, who was scared to death of Cornish, eventually made me the leader of our group. I didn't know what the hell I was expected to do. I always thought that since he knew I knew Cornish, he probably figured he was better off if he kept me on his side.

The sarge and I worked as a team. He would go out and get loaded, come in at 3:00 in the morning and scream, "Everybody up!"

It was my job to get our guys out of bed. That didn't do a lot for my popularity.

But I did have one incident I had to cover up.

One day near the end of basic, I'm checking out our barracks and I see two gay guys together and they aren't playing checkers, if you know what I mean. They're all over each other. There are a lot of things I have seen in my life, but this is not one I want to remember. It wasn't like taking in the Taj Mahal, if you want the truth. It was a Kodak moment with a twist.

I saw it and the other guy who was with me said, "You gotta report these guys."

Now, the first thing I thought of was, "Shit, if I turn these guys in, they're both gonna get dishonorable discharges and their lives are gonna be hell."

So, I told the guy I was with, "Keep your mouth shut and get lost. I'll handle this."

I went over and told the two guys to get dressed because we were gonna have a conversation. They did and I said to them, "Listen, I don't give a damn what you do, but as long as we're in this place, keep your hands off each other, understand?"

I added that if I caught them messing around again, I would tell the guys above us. We only had about three weeks of training left. We got through it and I never saw those guys wrapped up in each other again.

They kept their word to me.

In fact, the last I heard, they flew off to Hawaii and lived together. Hey, this was 1966. You couldn't admit you were gay. It was damn near like admitting you were a serial killer.

COPPOCK: Rock Hudson would have been enormously proud of you.

BUFFONE: (Laughing) Gosh, what a glowing tribute.

COPPOCK: I've got one more yarn to spin about Cornish that speaks volumes about him.

In '69, when you guys were just putrid, I mean 1–13 putrid, WBBM-TV Channel 2 hired Frank Leahy, the legendary Notre Dame football coach, to break down Bears games on Sunday night.

Leahy was so devoted to football that I swear he thought it was a notch above motherhood on the all-time list.

I remember Moose Krause, the long-time athletic director at ND, telling me at a banquet around '81 that he would beg Leahy to take vacations, only to see his suggestions fall on deaf ears.

Frank was so consumed by football that several ND alums have told me over the years that he was close to a nervous breakdown when he finally walked away from the job.

Leahy became appointment TV on Sunday nights for Bears fans and his favorite target, week in and week out was...hello...Frank Cornish.

I can still hear Leahy doing a voice-over on a play saying, "And there's number 73 [Cornish] cruising as usual." I guess we could say that Leahy was a bit sardonic. Deep inside, I think Frank looked at Cornish and said, "I know I could make this clown a football player."

BUFFONE: Ferdinand the Bull in pads.

COPPOCK: Packing a .38.

BUFFONE: (Laughing) What evil lurks in the mind of that man.

COPPOCK: How about pizza?

chapter 22

Battlin' Bears

COPPOCK: What is your pet peeve, the thing that makes you crazy?

BUFFONE: Don't try to embarrass me.

Ever.

If you beat me, that's fine, but don't make me look bad. You try that shit and I'll rip your goddamn throat out. I never let anybody make me look stupid.

I remember I clocked Paul Hornung my first or second year during a game against Green Bay. I left the Golden Boy on the sidelines. I knocked him out of the game after I gave him a stick right by our goal line.

Later that night I ran into Paul at a bar downtown and he said, "I can't believe I let a second-rate linebacker like you knock me out."

I told him, "Paul, you're lucky. I did you a favor." And I meant exactly what the hell I said.

COPPOCK: While the congregation sings Kumbaya, would you tell us why, after all these years, you remain a legend at Louisville's world famous Zanzibar Lounge?

BUFFONE: This isn't pretty.

Before my junior year at Louisville, I was sucking down beers in the Zanzibar when this big guy, he had to be a ridge runner, started glaring at me. A "ridge runner" is an expression used by the townies to explain the guys who came down from the Appalachians.

It was always said that they moved from "ridge to ridge." You didn't want to mess with these guys. Their idea of saying "please" was a left hook.

So this guy began staring at me and I know he wants a piece of me.

COPPOCK: How the hell can you blame this guy? You were just too damn pretty. He's waiting to haul his next truckload of moonshine while you're in the process of being chosen an All-American by the Associated Press and becoming the first player in Cardinals history to lead the team in tackles three consecutive years. Hell, I'd hate you too.

BUFFONE: This guy keeps glaring at me and finally I said to him, "Can I help you?"

Who the heck says that?

COPPOCK: WTF? Were you on a goodwill mission from the United Nations? This guy wanted to bust your skull because you're a student at Louisville with a dark complexion, high cheekbones, and a natural boyish charm. He probably had heard that every cheerleader on campus has told her sorority sisters that she'd shacked up with Doug Buffone.

You got it all going, and his biggest score in life was a moonshine hustle with another damn ridge runner. Of course he's staring at you. I assume the clown couldn't spell "dentist" if you spotted him five letters.

BUFFONE: Well, this guy started calling me "Pearly Teeth" and back in those days, I really did have nice teeth.

He kept hammering away about pearly teeth until he finally got up, walked over to me, and announced, "I'm gonna kick the shit out of you!"

Now the guy has really got me pissed off. I decided right then and there that I'm going to wipe the street with him. So I told the guy, "Alright, asshole, let's go outside."

COPPOCK: Did you lay the guy out?

BUFFONE: Lay the guy out? I think the son of a bitch might have been a distant cousin of Hercules. We wound up in the alley, and I'm telling you, I hit this guy with everything I had. I mean, I just whaled on him, but he wouldn't go down.

Son of a bitch! He must have been from a different planet.

Finally, the bar owner called the cops in to separate us or, I'm dead serious now, this guy might have killed me. I mean he might have left me dead.

COPPOCK: I hope to God you didn't ask this guy for a rematch.

BUFFONE: Of course I did. Being young and stupid, I told the bastard, "I'll meet you here again tomorrow, same time, same place." Well, the next day, I showed up, but "unfortunately" so did he. This guy had to be about 6'4" and he must have weighed 250 pounds. At the time, I was in at about 220 pounds.

This time around, I tried to box the guy and I did give him a bloody nose and a big welt on his forehead.

COPPOCK: Did the guy actually scare you?

BUFFONE: You're damn right he scared me. I mean, every time I hit him, I felt like I was hitting a wall. All I really remember is that he kept on saying, "I'm gonna bust you up, Pearly Teeth."

I thought I was fighting an animal. I never had a fight in the NFL that was even remotely close to the brawl I had with Goliath Boy.

The guy actually closed one of my eyes, he hit me so damn hard. My right hand was blown up from the punch I threw that hit him on the head.

Now, this will kill ya. I damn near challenged the guy to come back the next day for a third fight. I wanted to walk away on winner points. I thought I was invincible.

I knew Frank Camp, our head coach, was going to be ticked off when he saw me and he was. But Frank did take me to a campus doctor who gave me the good news that I didn't have any busted bones. I swear to God, that was the toughest fight I ever had.

COPPOCK: Vince Lombardi said, "I firmly believe that any man's finest hour, the greatest fulfillment of all he holds dear, is that moment he has worked his heart out and lies exhausted on the field of battle—victorious."

BUFFONE: That wouldn't have helped me a lick against Ridge Runner. You know what Lombardi says sounds great. But take a look at my career with the Bears. Fourteen years loaded with losses.

What the hell does, "Exhausted on the field of battle—a loser" mean?

It means you're disgusted, beyond angry. You hurt like hell. I had to learn during my career to just wipe out the scores. I didn't give a damn if we led by 40 or trailed by 40. I never took a play off. I mean that. When the games were over, I judged myself on what I had done as an individual. You know I've always had confidence in myself. Sure, there were times when I wanted to fight guys to take out my frustrations, but what good does that do?

Football fights are stupid. You tell me who wins when you throw a punch against a helmet?

Man on man never scared me. I mean not a damn bit. But some things are just crazy. One time, some whacko wanted me to jump out of an airplane.

I told him to ram it up his ass. I'm tough, but I'm not insane.

I hate to say this, but with the Bears, I finally accepted that things were just never gonna change.

So time and time again, I'd just ask myself about my personal performance: Did I drop back in coverage? Did I handle my assignments? Did I do anything to screw up our defense?

I had to challenge my game performances. Well, I had two interceptions, but I blew my assignments.

Nothing to be proud of here.

COPPOCK: I have no recollection, and I saw your entire 14-year career, of you ever really "free-lancing" or sacrificing a play to pad your numbers.

BUFFONE: Didn't happen. I never did that stuff. I'm proud of the fact that I finished with 24 career picks, the most ever by a Bears linebacker. I got those

Stop. Someone remind me about my blind side.
(Photo courtesy AP Images/NFL Photos)

picks because I did my job the right way. Screw the score. I couldn't change that.

It's how I kept my sanity. I couldn't let final scores define who I was or what I was all about.

COPPOCK: We now return to the adventures and misadventures of Douglas John Buffone outside the lines.

BUFFONE: Don't ask me why, but I always had a knack for doing weird shit. Every summer, there were county fairs all over Western Pennsylvania, home-baked pies, taffy apples, stuffed animals, the whole thing.

So, one year, I'm with some buddies and we go to the fair in Butler, about 45 minutes from Yatesboro. Well, the first thing I do is get into a Demolition Derby. You know, one of those crazy races where guys are just trying to bang the daylights out of each other.

I was driving a '53 Chevy.

That was no big deal. I survived.

But here's the killer.

As we're walking around the fair, I noticed this empty boxing ring. Are ya ready for this?

People were fighting a kangaroo, a trained kangaroo. Nuts, but true.

COPPOCK: What says fun like driving all over Western Pennsylvania in August to find a kangaroo to challenge your manhood? Who's next: Cleveland Williams, Zora Folley, or maybe Ernie Terrell?

BUFFONE: Exactly. Well, naturally, I've gotta take a shot at this animal. Keep in mind, kangaroo paws are sort of soft, but their feet are like sledgehammers.

Before we began the fight, the guy who was the kangaroo's manager, or whoever the hell he was, told me to put on a helmet. I also noticed that the goddamn kangaroo had boxing gloves on his feet and hands.

So the fight began and I'm trying to jab and do my best Muhammad Ali–type footwork. The damn kangaroo isn't buying in. This is a true story.

You thought that ridge runner was strong? Shit, he was nothing. He was a girl scout compared to this "thing."

The kangaroo kicked me in the stomach and knocked the living hell outta me. If he would have hit me six inches lower, there would have been no Buffone children.

The blow was so fuckin' powerful that it knocked me completely over the ring ropes and onto the ground. I think the fight lasted about 24 seconds.

I didn't wait around to see how the judges scored the bout.

COPPOCK: I'm trying to figure out your true personality. Your old man, Sam, seemed to be a guy who figured that fists were meant for two things: clutching coal and removing front teeth. His temper was legendary. You told us earlier that the word around Yatesboro was, "Don't screw around with Sam Buffone."

Now, you played tough, damn tough, but you weren't maniacal. You weren't Lyle Alzado. You were very much your father's son.

So why weren't you a bigger bad-ass when you played the Pack or the old Los Angeles Rams?

I'm not implying that you ever played soft. You were a man's man, but anybody who was raised by Sam Buffone, fought a damn ridge runner, and boxed a kangaroo figured to be a candidate to be institutionalized.

It's simple. You mastered controlled aggression.

BUFFONE: Hardly. I just stayed true to what I thought the game was all about. Sure, I had a few minor scraps. Again, I've never seen a helmet lose a fight to a hand.

In Louisville one summer, I went to a fair. I remember that a lot of guys were coming out of the mountains, "moonshiners," we called them, guys with hair like string, to see what was going on in the "big city."

So I climbed into the ring with a bear.

As you know, they're declawed and also muzzled.

COPPOCK: My sources have told me over the years that guys who trained wrestling bears used to tranquilize the poor things to bits. Do people still wrestle bears or has the ASPCA had it banned?

BUFFONE: Like the kangaroo, this wasn't pretty. The bear and I went back and forth, and finally like a nut, I tried to tackle the big S.O.B. He didn't move an inch. He didn't go anywhere.

COPPOCK: Sounds like the Old Man.

BUFFONE: Yeah, at contract time. He was the Papa Bear. If we went in with an agent, he had his claws out, ready to go for the throat. It was like the famous story of Vince Lombardi and the first time he was confronted by an agent who represented his All-Pro center, Jim Ringo.

They were looking for a salary increase.

Lombardi listened for a few minutes and then excused himself. He came back to the office a few minutes later and, legend has it, said, "Gentlemen, you're dealing with the wrong team. Jim Ringo no longer plays for the Packers. I just traded him to Philadelphia."

COPPOCK: It has been argued that the story wasn't really true but promoted by Lombardi to discourage other players from bringing in agents to help them land a higher salary.

BUFFONE: Makes sense. But Halas was like Lombardi. These guys did not part with their money easily. Hell, I had my best year and the Old Man wanted to give me a salary cut. I couldn't believe it. One year, he praised me up and down and offered me a contract "raise" for my performance.

I looked at it and said, "That's what I made last year."

Halas laughed and said, "The same salary is a raise."

God have mercy on my sanity.

COPPOCK: And what finally happened with the real bear?

BUFFONE: Finally, the bear just sat on me until I screamed "Uncle!" The moonshiners thought this was great stuff. They were laughing their asses off.

To answer the most obvious question, no, I was not drunk when I wrestled the bear. A couple of guys finally got the damn thing off me. That was the close of my storied career as a bear wrestler.

COPPOCK: If you hadn't had the skill to become an All-American or rack up 30 sacks from '67 through '69 with the Bears, is it even money you would have been a moonshiner or would you have preferred the more upscale life of a ridge runner?

BUFFONE: That's a tough and enlightened philosophical question.

Can I get back to you?

chapter 23

What Next? Life After the NFL

COPPOCK: Doug Buffone's last NFL game began at 12:33 PM EST in Philadelphia on December 23, 1979, against the Eagles. The colorful Red Cashion refereed the bout. Typical Bears, Walter Payton ran 84 yards for a touchdown on his first carry, but—there always had to be a "but" with the Bears in those days—the Payton scamper was called back on an illegal motion penalty assessed to Brian Baschnagel, the former Ohio State wideout who won the heart of Woody Hayes during his days with the Ohio State Buckeyes.

The Bears were 27–17 losers to Philly in that NFC wild-card game. It was the Eagles' first home-field postseason victory since Buck Shaw and the Eagles beat Vince Lombardi and Green Bay to win the NFL Championship 19 years earlier.

When Doug trudged off that God-awful carpet at old Veteran's Stadium, he knew it was his last hurrah.

Fourteen years with the Bears with only three winning seasons, plus two playoff appearances without a win.

You deserved a better fate, man.

BUFFONE: I know. I thought all about that stuff in the weeks after my last game.

I had two options: move on with the next phase of my life or sit around and drive myself nuts. It helped that I knew I was still going to do my share of radio shows and appearances. Plus, I still had the "Doug Buffone Chicago Bears Report."

I didn't feel left out by any means.

COPPOCK: I've got to mention this. I hated the Vet. The carpet in that stadium was the worst playing surface in the NFL.

BUFFONE: Like playing on concrete stuffed with broken glass.

COPPOCK: Tell that to Wendell Davis. Back in '93, Davis, a kid the Bears drafted No. 1 out of LSU in '88, leaped to make a catch on that two-bit surface. When he landed on the turf, he blew out the patella tendons in both his knees—not one—both.

The injury was a closed-case argument to ban Astro Turf.

Anyway, end of my sermon. Carry on, champ.

BUFFONE: The more I think about my career, I really could have played two more years, but let me tell you why I decided to walk.

My first marriage was done. We had separated. The divorce really did a number on me. I just couldn't maintain the concentration I needed to be able to play the level of football that I wanted to play.

I've already told you that Jim Finks wanted to re-up me for two more years, but here's what I've never told anybody. I just didn't feel mentally right. The divorce was keeping me up at night. Hell, I couldn't sleep.

I wasn't a nervous wreck, but I was damn close.

I'd always been a heavy smoker, but now I was smoking two packs of Marlboros a night. That's a night. I was lighting cigarettes off cigarettes.

You know, I left $300,000 on the table when I turned Finks down, but I knew what I had to do. I didn't want to go out there and embarrass myself. I already knew there were certain plays I just couldn't make anymore.

But to make matters worse, I knew at the time that my concentration level was shot.

COPPOCK: I also knew you had four major joints in operation: Sweetwater on Rush Street, the BBC and Hot Spurs in the same building on Division Street, and, of course, the Nickel Bag out in Schiller Park.

But come the fall of 1980 and you don't see checks coming from the Bears.

Was that financially jolting?

BUFFONE: Not really. It's what life's all about. You make adjustments and I did what I had to do to make things work financially.

Golden-voiced Paul Anka and I were partners in Las Vegas with a club called Jubilation.

I just feel damn lucky and blessed that I can look back on all four of those places and realize that I profited from all of them. You know, maybe I was destined to work the bar and restaurant business.

Let me tell you about a side gig I had in Louisville that lasted about two months. This would have been the summer of '65.

COPPOCK: Buckle up, sports fans, welcome to the world famous Pussy Cat A Go-Go. You know that sounds more like a third-rate strip joint than a singles bar, right?

BUFFONE: (Laughing) No, it was just your standard pickup joint. I worked the door before my senior year at Louisville to earn some extra money. I made about $3 an hour.

Sure, I had to put up with drunks and 16-year-old kids who'd walk in with phony IDs that said they were 28, but I really liked the work. Hell, it was fun.

Naturally, Frank Camp, my head coach at Louisville, got wind of what I was doing and told me I had to quit. I mean, he wouldn't bend an inch.

I told him, "I need the money," which I did, and Camp insisted, "I don't care how much money you need; you're not gonna take money from a place called the Pussy Cat A Go-Go .

COPPOCK: What, he wasn't big on pickup lines?

BUFFONE: (Laughing) Yeah, something like that.

I remember telling him that he couldn't make me quit since I was getting used to handling all the drunks. He still told me I had to get the hell out.

That was Frank.

During my four years at Louisville, I never got a dime in side money, not one damn nickel. Nothing!

I got $15 a month from the school that was called laundry money. But I never had a booster come in and slip me a couple of hundred bucks after I'd had a big Saturday afternoon.

Not once.

Basketball was a different story. We had guys on campus who were wheeling around in expensive cars. I never asked about it. Frankly, I didn't care.

By the way, the basketball team at Louisville found out I was a "player." Hey, my jump shot was real. So, I go to a practice to see if I can actually play some hoops. Well, the fact is I couldn't. I got matched up in the pivot with a guy by the name Wes Unseld, a guy who later won the NBA MVP award and Rookie of the Year in his first season with the Baltimore Bullets. Big old Wes just knocked me out of the park.

Anyway, as regards money, I still had my '57 Chevrolet. If you know a damn thing about cars, you know that baby was hot. I loved that ride. It had a 327 engine that just roared. I think my old man and I paid about a grand for that car.

When I joined the Bears, I bumped it up a notch. I bought a new Chevy Impala for just under $3,000. Think about that. You can't buy a transmission today for three large.

COPPOCK: It seems funny to me that we go back about 45 years and we've never talked about this. Back in the early 70s when you had the Nickel Bag out in Schiller Park, I never recall you being there during the football season.

I just have no recollection of you dancing up a storm on Tuesday night during a game week.

BUFFONE: Nope. I pledged allegiance to pro football. I knew pro football was what got me into the Nickel Bag in the first place. The guys I invested with wanted me there seven nights a week and I couldn't blame them.

I was in my late twenties and I played for the Chicago Bears. I had established a pretty big name in town. They didn't see me as a guy who was gonna wash dishes or tend bar. They put me in the deal because of my name value.

They wanted the people coming in to see Doug Buffone.

But during the football season, I only went there on Sundays after ballgames.

COPPOCK: Did you ever get in a fight with some boozed-up clod who thought he could kick the hell out of Doug Buffone?

BUFFONE: Just once.

One night, this guy walks in the place and he started demanding that our doorman tell him where I was because he wanted to kick the shit out of me. Well, the guy at the door did exactly what he should have done. He told him I wasn't there, despite the fact that I was sitting about 20 feet away.

Anyway, my guy comes over and said to me, "There's a drunk at the door who wants to kick the shit out of you. What do you want me to do?"

I told him, "Send the guy over!"

So, this guy walks up and says, "Are you Doug Buffone?"

I said, "Yeah."

He glared at me and said, "So you're the big tough football player…I'm gonna kick the shit out of you right here."

I tried to play the nice guy role.

I told him, "I don't want any trouble. C'mon just relax and let me buy you a beer."

Now, the guy says to me, "Fuck you!"

Well, that was it. Now I'm pissed off. So I told the guy, "Let's go outside, just you and me."

We went outside and I just kicked the crap outta that son of a bitch. It was like a linebacker going one on one with a placekicker. I buried him.

That was the only time I ever decked a guy at one of my places.

Really, I was lucky.

I never had that many guys who walked up and wanted to get a rep by busting me up. I'm not saying it never happened because it did, but not nearly as many times as you might think.

COPPOCK: We have to put this in the mix. You know there are some people out there, a very small minority, who truly believe that you had to be involved with the "Boys," the wise guys, since you've had your hands in as many places as you did over the years.

BUFFONE: I understand that. It goes with the territory. My last name ends with a vowel, so I'm already under suspicion.

But let me tell you how it worked. I never got social with any of those guys. But if you're going to be in the restaurant business or own a bar, or both, you learn pretty quickly how certain things work.

The jukeboxes and the linens did come from the wise guys. It was just the way things were done. But I can tell you with a conscience that's clear as hell that nobody ever tried to shake me down and I never got involved on a personal level with any of those guys.

Halas gave me some damn good advice when he heard that I had opened up the Nickel Bag. He told me, "Doug, remember something. You can't hide out from those guys."

You know Halas had his security people keep an eye on me.

The Feds in Chicago were eyeing me as well as the NFL because of Joe Namath and his partners who'd opened Bachelors III. That was the place Joe had in Manhattan. From day one, the joint picked up a reputation as a hangout for the mob.

Maybe the "goodfellas" were star-struck.

I almost died laughing when Joe said he was going to quit pro football because Commissioner Rozelle was going to force him to unload his interest in Bachelors. That's like Steve Dahl threatening to open his own disco. It was pure crap. Namath wasn't ever going to quit.

Hell, he'd just won Super Bowl III. He was making more money in a day with commercial work than guys were making in a season.

But never forget this. Namath had backed Rozelle into a corner.

Joe knew there were known gamblers and wise guys in his bar, but he also knew he was so damn big at that time that the league couldn't afford to lose him. It would be like taking the singing out of *The Sound of Music* or Marlon Brando out of *The Godfather*. You can't do it.

Plus, the TV networks would have gone out of their minds.

I'll guarantee you that Rozelle heaved a sigh of relief when Joe finally agreed to walk away from his bar.

The Feds I dealt with were really hysterical. They came in and asked me, "Who do you know?" And I said, "Nobody." They kept on pressing me and I kept on telling them that they were full of shit. They were trying to scare me by telling me they were going to "stay" on me. Anyway, they finally came back about six weeks later and said they hadn't found a thing.

I told 'em, "Gee, that's a shock. What did I tell you?"

COPPOCK: You know the 1960s really represented a time of social change in America. But the '70s were, in their own way, just as radical. It was like the hippies went uptown.

In the summer of '74, one of the hottest joints in America had to be the Bombay Bicycle Club, the BBC, which was your new place on Division Street.

BUFFONE: God, the BBC just took off. The place was unreal. It was so much a part of the whole John Travolta *Saturday Night Fever* era.

We packed that place every night. I remember Priscilla Presley, Elvis' ex, used to stop in all the time.

Our appeal wasn't to the hippies. We delivered an upscale crowd that was willing to spend money. Really the whole culture on Rush Street and Division was going through a sweeping change.

COPPOCK: I practically lived at the BBC during that opening summer. I'd have dinner at Hot Spurs, the joint you ran on the first floor on Division, just west of State, and then slide upstairs to the BBC.

It was really one heck of a one-two punch.

I also remember that guys and girls just dressed to kill. I don't know how many times I stopped at the old Davis for Men, a boutique on Wells Street, to get a new Nik-nik body shirt to wear that night at BBC.

But clothes weren't the only change in that era. The drug culture had graduated from weed to blow. Cocaine arrived with a flourish in '74.

About the drugs. I'll tell the truth if you will. I tried coke twice and then walked away from it.

Let me tell you why. The high was so prolific, so gosh darn good that it perfectly fed my addictive personality. I walked away because if I ended up hooked, I figured my septum would cave in.

BUFFONE: I never did cocaine. I was at a party once and there was a mound of the white powder on a table and people were snorting like crazy. Somebody passed the bowl to me and I said, "No thanks, I just don't do this stuff."

So the bowl came around a second time and people were on me to give my nostrils a workout and I told 'em again, "No, I just don't need this."

Well, the guy who had bought the coke got angry with me. He was telling me how expensive the shit was. I said, "Screw it, I don't care."

I have never smoked marijuana. I never did cocaine. That doesn't make me a saint. I just didn't wanna mess around with the stuff.

I do recall that in the mid-'70s, Rush Street began to change. Do you remember the cops on horseback? They were there because while the street was still about boy-girl attraction, it had gotten a little too dangerous for its own good.

I remember when we had Sweetwater, the forerunner to Gibson's; it was a restaurant in an association with the other places on Rush Street and State, along with Division. We all wanted to hire our own private security. There was no doubt that the influence of cocaine had something to do with Rush Street becoming too hostile for its own good.

Narcs were talking to waiters and waitresses all over the area. The undercover cops weren't after them; they wanted to find out who the big money players were. The pushers were pretty easy to spot; they were the ones who were always leaving the big tips.

COPPOCK: That atmosphere flew in the face of Harry Caray, the masterful play-by-play man, declaring himself the "Mayor of Rush Street." He didn't need coke to soar. He was his own rocket ship. He was Armstrong on the moon.

Man, I can't wait to hear the yarn about why you stopped drinking.

BUFFONE: You'll love this. Around 1976, Artis Gilmore tries to walk in to the BBC. Now we had an air-tight rule—you had to have an ID to get in any of our places. But, y'know, sometimes you have to make exceptions. Our guys at the door asked Artis for his ID and he didn't have one. So my rocket scientists told Artis he couldn't come in. Oh God, guess what happens? One of the local newspapers writes a story about Gilmore being denied entry to BBC. However, here is the real issue. Every damn story about Artis didn't just call it "the BBC," outlets were going with "Doug Buffone's BBC."

I'm at training camp and I see the story. I went nuts. I tried to hide every paper I could find, so our black players wouldn't think I was a racist. I was really in shock. So, I reached out to guys I knew in the press and they took me off the hook. I owe them. Meanwhile, I fired the two clods who told Artis, who had to be 7'8" with his afro, to get lost.

chapter 24

What? Mike Ditka Quotable?

COPPOCK: Something's wrong. I mean really off-base. I haven't seen or heard anything outrageous from Mike Ditka in at least three hours. The mythical Chicago Bear is quite simply the most cussed and discussed figure in Chicago sports history. Put it this way, the quotes of Chicago sports legends Ernie Banks, Ron Santo, Michael Jordan, Dennis Rodman, Bobby Hull, Stan Mikita, and for gosh sakes, Yukon Moose Cholak combined haven't filled one-tenth the notebooks that Ditka has filled with his rants and one-liners. No NFL coach has ever meant "showbiz" quite like the septuagenarian from Aliquippa, P.A.

A few days before Seattle hiccupped the Super Bowl to New England, Ditka appeared on HBO's award-winning *Real Sports* to discuss himself, the '85 Bears, and just where the game of football is going. Now, let's keep this in mind, Ditka came out of the same Western Pennsylvania region that spawned Doug Buffone and countless other football giants.

Mike has become a millionaire at least 15 times over through his long association with the Bears and the NFL. If Mike isn't hustling booze, he's selling a magic potion to cure erectile dysfunction. At the risk of sounding, shall we say trite, I once said at a banquet that if murder were ever legalized in the United States, Ditka might turn up on the tube telling his legions of admirers, "Isn't it time you had a killing at your 4th of July barbecue?" Cute? Maybe.

Iron Mike Ditka—we used to beat the hell out of each other in practice.

Ditka told Bryant Gumbel on *Real Sports* that if he had an eight-year-old kid today, he wouldn't let him play football. Does that make Mike, a guy who earns about $35,000 a speech because of his link to the game, a hypocrite?

BUFFONE: No! No way. Now, Mike might change his mind if he had a kid who could run the forty in 4.4. I know I would. I think what Mike is really thinking about is the game we played back in the '60s and '70s and I'm sure he's looking at how many of the '85 Bears are going through hell. If I had an eight-year-old kid and I really thought he wanted to play, that his heart was really into it, I'd tell him to do it.

But, that's me.

My son, Doug Jr., played football at Loyola Academy. He was good enough to get a partial ride to Miami of Ohio to play ball. The kid blew out a knee his freshman year and that ended his career. It also meant he lost his scholarship money, which sucks. The kids get tossed in the garbage if they can't play. I never went overboard encouraging Doug to play football. I just told him when he came to me and said he wanted to play that he had to go all out; he couldn't go halfway.

You know one day when Doug was playing for Loyola, he just didn't get up after a play. Ten guys got up and he stayed on the ground. I ran like hell down to the locker-room to see what was wrong with him. It turned out that he had a detached retina. I remember saying to myself, "I love this game, but I hate this game." In some ways, I probably felt his injury was my fault. I had another son, Ryan, who attended Fenwick. He gave football a shot, but told me, "Dad, I just don't think this is where I fit. I want to play tennis." I told him that was great.

I've often wondered over the years how my sons would have been treated if I'd moved back to Yatesboro after my days with the Bears. You know where I grew up, if you had any talent, you got 50 lashes if you didn't suit up. Now, toss in the fact that I was an NFL player. I think it would have been rough—miserable for my kids.

Listen, this game can be hell. That reminds me of Marc Trestman in 2014 saying the Bears were "in a good place" after they got beat by the Packers and New England by something like 120 points.

COPPOCK: Don't be a hard-ass. The Bears gave up 51 in Foxboro to the Pats and 55 at Green Bay seven days later.

BUFFONE: Trestman's comment was the single dumbest comment in Chicago Bears history. It was beyond stupid. Good place? When a guy came into our studio and told me what Trestman said, my first reaction was, "What's a good place? Hell?"

God, the players just walked all over Trestman.

You've seen a lot of lousy Bears teams. Which one is your all-time worst?

COPPOCK: Abe's 1973 Bears went 3–11. They were just putrid, but I'm also going to mention the 2014 Bears for this reason. The club had no guts, no energy. They were all phonies like Jared Allen waving at the crowd and Jay Cutler pouting. They also had three linebackers who couldn't play.

So, despite a glowing 5–11 mark, I'm going to declare the 2014 Bears the worst sideshow in team history. Briggs blows off practice to open a restaurant, Brandon Marshall turned clueless and gutless, and Jay Cutler will leave Chicago as the most hated athlete in the history of our fair city.

And, of course, Chris Conte couldn't play a full game.

BUFFONE: Are you done? Okay, listen up. The Bears will be in the Super Bowl by 2018. Why? Because John Fox won't put up with any crap. He's a throwback guy. I think he believes in my philosophy. You run the ball, you stop the ball, and you pressure the quarterback.

COPPOCK: I buy that—lock, stock, and hip pads. Lee Corso, the ESPN football guru, told me years ago when he was at Indiana that he had a three-pronged concept on how to win: defense, an offensive line and—this is big—the kicking game.

BUFFONE: Here's something else John Fox will do. He'll develop a mindset with the Bears that they have to play to keep their jobs. He won't put up with a guy taking a series off because he's outta breath or has a sore ankle.

Fox has to change the mindset, the culture, and I really believe in George McCaskey. I think George will leave John and his staff alone. George is a smart guy. I don't doubt for a second that 2014 left him sick to his stomach.

So, now he has to do what Halas did with Finks over 40 years ago. He has to back off, run the business end with Ted Phillips, and let Ryan Pace and Fox clean up the football operation.

COPPOCK: Fox got sold down the river by John Elway in Denver. There's a reason why the Broncos suffered down the stretch and in the playoffs. Peyton Manning just could not air the ball out. He couldn't throw deep. He was hurt. Hey, he's been in the NFL since Bronko Nagurski for God's sake.

Fox knew by late November that he had to change the team's culture. He knew Denver had to become run-oriented, but they didn't have the pieces. Did you see Peyton versus the Colts in the playoffs? My daughter could have thrown the ball with more zip.

BUFFONE: Looking down the road, let me tell you something else the Bears need. Think about Olin Kreutz, the center. The guy was a natural leader. He was the sheriff on a lot of Bears teams. The '85 Bears had about seven sheriffs.

chapter 25

The Wife Is Always Right

COPPOCK: Okay, what say we all pour a double shot of Jack Daniels before we begin this next dance? Or maybe a good old-fashioned Whiskey Sour?

Better yet, go ahead and sip the slop yourself.

This doesn't qualify either Doug or me for sainthood, but let the record show that Buff hasn't touched a drop in well over 25 years, while I've gone 30-plus without the sauce.

BUFFONE: When I joined the Bears in '66, there was so much damn drinking going on that a guy could be forgiven for thinking half the club brought hip flasks to practice.

COPPOCK: That's what the fans do on frigid December Sundays, or for that reason, 89 degree nights in August.

BUFFONE: There was a heck of a lot more drinking in the NFL when I broke in than there is in the league today.

I don't know why. Maybe, we just had more time on our hands since there was no internet or cell phones. Who knew there was going to be something called YouTube? Also, today's players are far more concerned about what they eat and drink than we were. When I broke in back in '66, nutrition was a joke. We loaded up on pasta, pancakes, potatoes, bread, biscuits, and ice cream.

Who knew what a freakin' carb was? Today it has a different name.

Diabetes.

COPPOCK: The booze part was highly legit. There were more rogues in the league when you joined the party back in 1966. The league was far more colorful. I remember Paul Hornung telling me that after practices with Vince Lombardi up in Green Bay that he'd go back to his apartment with his friends and make a pitcher of martinis to loosen up.

After being on the field with Lombardi, the boys went sailing at Paul's place. After an hour, they were all happily redefining "Blitz!"

BUFFONE: I wasn't with the Bears long before I learned that booze was a big part of the team culture. Doug Atkins took me out to a shit-kicker bar to listen to some country and western music a few weeks into my first season.

Doug could put 'em away like no man I have ever seen before or since. I think he drank about 19 martinis that night. I tried to keep up with Doug, which was idiotic. I wound up on the floor, just screaming for help.

I thought my head was gonna split in half. I think I just fell apart after my 14th martini.

COPPOCK: I remember you and the guys going to joints like the Cottage and the Ivanhoe after practice. They were both close to Wrigley Field and both very player-friendly.

BUFFONE: Listen, there wasn't a bar on the North Side where we didn't drink.

COPPOCK: I got one you won't remember. In October 1972, with Abe Gibron at the helm, you guys played and beat the Vikings in a Monday night game at Soldier Field 13–10. The victory lifted your record to a dazzling 2–3–1.

I have this distant memory of several Bears trying to put Abe on their shoulders after the final gun before quickly realizing it would have been easier to move the Hancock Building to South Bend.

Following the game, a bunch of your guys turned up at a bar on Diversey Parkway to celebrate. The joint had a 2:00 AM license, so around 1:45, my roommate, a guy named Harry Nutter, got a novel idea. He said, "Why don't we invite the players over to our joint?"

We brought about four cases of beer and about a dozen guys stopped by the brownstone we had on Oakdale Street west of Halsted.

I have a couple of memories from that night.

About 3:00 in the morning, Butkus noticed that some towing service was ready to lift his Corvette. Dick was parked illegally in a residential parking lot, but so what?

Crunch ran out and threatened to beat the hell outta the guy who was gonna tow his ride. The guy very meekly, dripping "survival" from all pores, backed off.

Dick had that effect on people. Butkus would have made Mussolini cringe.

BUFFONE: Can we dim the house lights and begin to tell the congregation just why I stopped drinking?

COPPOCK: This is classic. The stunningly attractive damsel of Goose Creek, South Carolina, wins by knockout over one of the toughest guys who ever played in the NFL.

BUFFONE: I was always a vodka guy. Vodka and martinis. One night, Dana and I were sitting at the bar at Sweetwater. You know I loved the bar we had there, but I never liked the food. The menu was too French, too chichi.

Well, I'm drinking non-stop. I mean, I'm ramrod stiff. I know I had downed about 15 martinis, maybe more. With each drink, my wife was getting more and more agitated with me. While Dana is very loving, she's also fiery.

My wife, Dana—the most wonderful lady in the world.

She was big-time pissed. We finally left the bar and drove home. Dana was so damn mad that she couldn't see straight. She knew exactly what to do with me for the rest of the night.

I wound up sleeping on the coach.

COPPOCK: That's not so bad. What guy hasn't slept on the couch at least once during a marriage? If I'd been Dana, I would have made you sleep at a bus stop.

BUFFONE: Hold on, it gets worse. While I'm passed out on the couch, Dana called up the Sweetwater, flexed her muscles, and fired our bartender, John Pondarelli. She hollered at John for serving me when I was obviously dead drunk.

She did all this for love, her devotion to me.

That's Dana.

Pondarelli called me a few hours later and asked me what he should do. I told him, "John, don't worry. Your job is safe. Dana's just pissed at me because I got loaded."

But I got the message.

That was the last time I ever had a drink. I just walked away from the stuff.

COPPOCK: Massive steaks, huge slabs of carrot cake, and other foot-high desserts, along with dealmakers and a seemingly endless flock of celebrities. That, my friend, was and is the quickie summation of the legendary Gibson's Steak House on Rush Street.

Frank Sinatra loved the place. Dennis Rodman used to be a regular. It's been a "must" for Billy Joel when he's come to Chicago. Derek Jeter used to come in for lunch whenever the Yankees were in town to play the White Sox.

Doug had "points" in Gibby's. He wouldn't reveal what kind of coin the place pays him on an annual basis, but he would say, "It's a very comfortable annuity."

Gibson's replaced Sweetwater at the high-end corner of Rush and Bellevue Streets (Frank Sinatra Place). Old Blue Eyes used to sit at Table 61 in Gibson's, where he'd hold court with his comic sidekick, Tom Dreesen, Harry Caray, and more than just a handful of wise guys.

One tip about the ultra-stylish restaurant: bring plastic. You'll need it. There are no $3 cheeseburgers.

Did I mention that Aerosmith lead singer Steven Tyler, used to love to walk into the place unannounced?

Did I tell you that the martinis damn near required a drinker to wear a life preserver?

BUFFONE: The transition from Sweetwater to Gibson's happened very rapidly. The partners all got together to have a meeting about what we were going to do with the place. We knew that we had the best damn location in the city, but we felt like something was lacking.

Let me tell you what it was.

Our bar just hopped, but we felt that we were losing business because our food wasn't that good.

It was Sid Luckman, one of our partners, who introduced the oversized desserts.

COPPOCK: Sid was always larger than life. Really a 100 percent man's man. My ex-wife Anna Marie and I were in there on a brutally cold night in 1982. I was still drinking, so I warmed up at the bar with three or four drinks before settling into dinner. After the meal, I told Anna the food was just too damn rich.

It must have been the French "touch."

BUFFONE: Here's an inside story for you. At first, the partners thought about opening a burger joint. That was actually our first plan of attack. But we finally decided that the way to go was with big steaks. We wanted a pronounced Midwestern feel and felt that steaks would be the key.

You know, during the 25 years Gibson's has been around, it has been frequently listed as one of the 20 highest grossing restaurants in America.

COPPOCK: I was thumbing through a magazine the other day that listed Gibson's revenues at just over $22 million.

Jeez, in 1981 Eddie Einhorn and Jerry Reinsdorf bought the White Sox—an entire franchise—for about $19,000,000.

BUFFONE: You know what's funny? Everybody thinks I met Frank at Gibson's because he came in there on a frequent basis. But I actually met Sinatra with Jack McHugh (powerhouse Chicago businessman) at the old Four Torches on Armitage. I also saw Frank a couple of times in Vegas.

COPPOCK: Gibson's began the new revolution on Rush Street.

This didn't happen overnight, but joints for young singles eventually gave way over the years to pricey restaurants that weren't looking to dish out Miller Lites to 22-year-old kids from Bolingbrook.

For me, Gibson's replaced the Palm over on East Lake Shore Drive as the place to be seen.

God, back in the early '80s, the Palm was beyond red hot. They had great food, a friendly bar, and Johnny Blandino, a fabulous maître d'. Blandino knew everybody. The guy had a steel-trap memory. Plus, he used to love to drink with his customers.

When the Palm began to fade in the late '80s, Gibson's—named for the Gibson martini—became the be-seen restaurant in Chicago.

It still is.

Johnny Blandino was just great, and so is Gibson's boss Steve Lombardo and John Colletti. You can't help but love him. If I go to Gibson's and don't see them, I get ticked off.

Look at Rush Street today. The kid's game is over. Gibson's is part of what's affectionately referred to as the Viagra Triangle, a reference to high-end businessmen who flock to Gibby's as well as the other elite establishments that have flooded the area over the years.

Ya know Doug, Rush Street ain't the Rush Street that we grew up with back in the '60s and '70s. Today, you just see too damn many 70-year-old guys in custom-made suits trying to hustle 24-year-old up-and-coming advertising chicks and babes who are trying to carve a niche in the fashion industry. And, last but not least, young ladies are just dying to land a guy with an unlimited bankroll.

BUFFONE: Chester, no argument from me.

I'm just glad I'm no longer sleeping on that damn couch.

chapter 26

The Wrigley Field Rat Race

BUFFONE: You know, when I first joined the Bears, we practiced and played at Wrigley Field. The conditions were less than ideal. If you didn't get in the shower within 10 minutes after a ballgame, I swear the water was ice cold.

COPPOCK: Let me give the folks at home a quick rundown. The Bears shared locker-room facilities with the Cubs down the left-field line. The door opened right by the foul pole. The place was so damned cramped that I always said that if a con at Cook County Jail had filed suit claiming a Human Rights Violation, the sucker probably would have won. You guys were like a bag of pretzels. I sure as hell remember the shower.

It was so damn crowded that I used to tell myself, heaven forbid if a guy drops a bar of soap. I mean, you never know, right?

BUFFONE: You want more? The bathroom stalls were practically on top of each other. Guys used to light matches to get rid of the smell. It was brutal.

We also had just one weight machine. The damn thing had about five settings to do various exercises. How in the hell are 40 players gonna build up muscle mass with that kind of shit?

That's where Clyde Emerich comes in. Halas brought him in to be our strength coach.

The beloved Old Man. It was an honor to host George Halas at Sweetwater. (I've since burned those pants.)

COPPOCK: Great guy. Great motivator. His presence actually moved the club's weight training into the 20th century.

BUFFONE: You're right. At first, since Wrigley Field was so damn out of touch, Clyde got guys to go to the Irving Park YMCA to lift weights. We also played racquetball. I used to shower after practice at Cubs Park and go lift at the Y.

COPPOCK: Early on at Green Bay, Lombardi was preaching isometrics. Give me 15,000 words on why you thought that was a complete waste of time.

BUFFONE: It was. When I joined the Bears, guys would stand and press against the wall and groan like they were killing themselves. Hell, they weren't doing a thing. Those guys had what we called "milk muscles."

COPPOCK: You know Tom Thayer just loves to romanticize about the Bears at Wrigley Field. I really like Thayer. Tom was a terrific football player, a rugged left guard on the '85 world champions, and he's developed into a great color announcer on Bears broadcasts.

I love to tell Tom about Halas vs. Lombardi and the south end zone that was only eight yards long at the east end because it happened to merge with the visitors' dugout. But my God, the crowds were just fuckin' raucous. Wild.

The loudest single turnout I ever heard at a Bears game wasn't at Soldier Field during the Ditka era. No way. It was November 17, 1963, when the Old Man and the Bears—on their way to an NFL title—just blasted Green Bay 26–7. The noise was shrill. I thought the crowd noise was going to blow the roof onto Clark Street.

God bless the Old Man. He busted the city fire code sky high. Halas used to add so many extra seats where the Cubs had box seats that getting to a hot dog stand could take a light year. I remember the north end zone where the left-field wall was about six inches away from the end line.

The place made no sense, but God it had charm. However, let the record show that rival players used to pack soap because they complained that Halas wouldn't leave any. A myth? I doubt it.

BUFFONE: Let me tell you what else the joint featured. What says fun like rats? My second year with the Bears, my job was to bring donuts to the Saturday morning walk-through. I showed up one day and this fuckin' rat who had to weigh 30 pounds confronts me.

I tried to stare him down, but he wasn't going to give an inch. Finally, I said this isn't worth it, so I just threw the donuts away. About 10 seconds later, 50 rats converged on the damn things.

COPPOCK: I can relate to that. In '75, I was in my second year doing public address for the Bears at Soldier Field for a whopping $100 a game. That was up from $35 the year before, where I actually did play by play walking up and down the visitor's sideline. Really, ya can't make this stuff up. There I was, 26 years old, doing P.A. for the legendary Chicago Bears, and I'm standing on the 25-yard line trying to tell the audience who made the tackle on plays that happened 60 yards away.

I was also a sportscaster at WISH-TV in Indianapolis at the time. So I was commuting 360 miles round-trip to tell people that Bobby Douglass or Bob Avellini had just thrown incomplete to whomever. One evening, you guys were playing a Monday night game against the Vikings. I had a ball watching Howard Cosell voice his halftime highlights. Howard didn't have a thing written down. He just sailed right through the package in one take.

The guy was a master. Seeing Howard do his thing was about the only fun I had.

I got to my perch above the old west press box about 90 minutes before the game and did what I always did, run a mic check. I clicked the sucker on and there was no sound. We didn't get any sound until the second half. Later that night, one of the park district guys who worked at the stadium told me rats had chewed their way through the wires. By the way, while I was doing P.A. for you guys, the biggest cheer I usually got was when I announced the two-minute warning to the end of the ballgame.

What can I say? We lived life in the big city.

chapter 27

Just Sayin'

COPPOCK: To truly understand Doug Buffone, you have to know his quirky language, heretofore known as "Dougisms."

His down-home take-no-prisoners method of discussing either the 50-yard line or peace in the Middle East is usually littered with his favorite phrases.

Take copious notes, class. There will be a quiz.

The Country Club Division:

20. "Get your head out of your ass!" Can be applied to virtually any quarterback the Bears have had since the glory days of Luckman.

19. "I'd rather spend a weekend in jail than a day in training camp." A warm and fuzzy tribute to the two-a-day drills that Abe Gibron mercilessly ran during his tour of duty as coach of the Monsters of the Midway.

18. "He couldn't play dead." A natural and friendly reference to any ballplayer who really shouldn't be on the 53-man roster. Is that you out there, Kordell Stewart?

17. "You can't run a donkey and expect to win the Kentucky Derby." Just check out the list of first-round busts the Bears have drafted over the years and you'll have a complete grasp on that statement.

The Black Tie Gala Division:

16. "Kiss my ass and call it a love story." A warm, friendly refrain to any first-time caller who actually thinks he knows more about the game than D.B. or O.B.

15. **"Your sidewalk doesn't go all the way to the street."** A glowing tribute to the years that John Shoop ran the Bears offense. Shoop was as imaginative as an amoeba. His idea of wide-open football was a shovel pass on third-and-26.
14. **"He's as soft as a grape."** If you need help with this one, go watch replays of a Christian Slater movie.
13. **"The guy tried to make a necklace out of my teeth."** Don't ask me why, but this makes me think of Charlie Sanders or Larry Csonka.

Dana and I discussing the 6-4-3 with Tommy Lasorda, the man who wanted me to be a Dodger.

The $62.00 Filet Mignon Division

12. **"Hey, pal, I didn't play the piano for 14 years; I played in the National Football League."** Reserved for callers who need to be reminded that Doug Buffone was not your average NFL employee.
11. **"He's a card."** Could mean he's just a funny guy or, perhaps, laconically used to suggest that guy doesn't know what day it is.
10. **"I could find better players after midnight on Rush Street."** This may be used to describe the quarterbacking brilliance of Rusty Lisch, the former Notre Dame signal caller. To suggest his anemic play aggravated his teammates is a massive understatement. Legend has it that after one Bears loss, Dan Hampton had to be restrained from attacking Lisch.
9. **"Pissing up a rope."** Buffone quoting head coach Jack Pardee about what life was like with the Bears (or any other inept team) before he left the club after the 1977 season.

The Gibson's Restaurant and Martini Division:

8. **"I'll jump down your throat and tap dance on your lungs."** A subtle way of saying, "Welcome to the NFL, punk!"
7. **"Thanks, little buddy."** A pointed reminder from Buffone when it's your turn to pick up the check.
6. **"It's football, mister."** An explanation to his radio show callers who are having trouble understanding why a running back's helmet was sent flying into the upper deck at Soldier Field.
5. **"A rag-arm quarterback."** In the immortal words of Abe Gibron to Bobby Douglass, "Throw the ball you dumb donkey."

The All-Halas All the Time Division:

4. **Jeopardy answer: "Dumb as a rock."** Question: What is the offensive knowledge of Lovie Smith?
3. **"I'll rip off your arm and show it to you."** The Dick Butkus School of Business.
2. **"Here's the killer."** Pay attention, here.
1. **"Just."** Always added for emphasis in almost every sentence.

Just sayin'….

chapter 28

Can't We All Just Get Along?

COPPOCK: On the sixth day of August 2014, Buffone had a downcast expression as I met him at his residence to strike up our latest gabfest.

I have seen that expression too many times in the past. He's an emotional Italian. He's passionate about everything he loves.

His expression is a visual reminder that No. 55 is still, after all these years, yearning to know what the Bears "might" have been if George Halas had tossed the reins to his brilliant young assistant coach, George Allen, after the Bears won a world title in 1963.

That is the same Allen who also scored Gale Sayers and Dick Butkus in the 1965 NFL draft, the greatest one-two swipe in "selection process" history. Somehow, some way, the New York Giants, in the midst of a string of losing seasons, took Auburn running back Tucker Frederickson with the first pick. San Francisco followed up with Ken Willard, a fullback out of North Carolina, at two.

That left Allen drooling as he grabbed Butkus at three and the Comet with the fourth overall choice.

I asked Buffone about the wunderkind coach.

BUFFONE: I should have had George Allen as my head coach, something I could only dream about.

You know, maybe Halas feared Allen. Maybe the Old Man knew that if he gave George his job that Allen would have wanted to do a complete house cleaning. Allen wouldn't have wanted Sid Luckman hanging around. I have no doubt that guys like Luke Johnsos and Phil Handler all would have been given the axe, too.

Plus, and this is huge, Allen would have dealt with agents. He was pragmatic that way, and he saw the future of pro football representation. The revolution was on. Players throughout the league were getting savvy about their contracts and finding lawyers to boost their take.

Allen knew that if the Old Man had one glaring weakness, it was the fact that he was just too damn loyal. Halas just had too many guys on his staff who were pals more than they were coaches.

But this wasn't 1956.

COPPOCK: Didn't September 27, 1970, tell you something about just how the Papa Bear operated?

BUFFONE: Absolutely. We were playing the Eagles at old Dyche Stadium (now Ryan Field) up in Northwestern. And, funny thing was, we actually won the ballgame. But what became apparent to us as players during the game was that Halas was sending down plays from upstairs to Jim Dooley, our head coach.

Think about that.

The guy was 75 years old and he was sending down plays to the sidelines. Talk about old school. The Old Man, bless him, probably still had a Model T in his garage.

Can you imagine Halas wearing the "uniforms" coaches wear today to sell NFL apparel? I laugh when I think about the Old Man wearing a Bears hoodie or a team stocking cap.

COPPOCK: Halas was meant to wear his trademark fedora with an off-gray overcoat. I could never see the Old Man wearing a league-approved Bears warm-up jacket. Honestly, I'd just kill to see Halas wearing an officially licensed Lance Briggs windbreaker.

BUFFONE: Please! Even after he left coaching, Halas was always in control, at least until Jim Finks took over as GM in '74. He was like Lombardi; he just couldn't retire. It drove him nuts.

COPPOCK: I'll raise you. Go back to December 1956. The Bears were just out and demolished by the New York Giants 47–7 in the league's 24th annual NFL title game at old Yankee Stadium.

The party was over five minutes after the kickoff. Maybe five minutes before the coin toss. At halftime with the Bears bleeding 34–7, Halas came raging down to the locker-room and he spent the entire second half on the sidelines berating his players.

The late Bill Bishop, a hard-nosed defensive tackle from North Texas State, told me years ago that the night before the game, Halas just drained the heart and soul from his club. Paddy Driscoll was the team's head coach. But that didn't stop the Old Man from getting in his best shot.

Halas told the guys at their meeting following dinner that they were going to be playing on national TV the following day and he didn't want to see any dirty play, no cheap shots. He wanted them to be "professional."

I also heard that later that night he fined Rick Casares, his bread and butter fullback, $500 for arriving about three minutes late for curfew. Christ, Rick was having dinner with his mother.

Casares was the best big back in the NFL.

He had just rushed for nearly 1,200 yards playing a 12-game schedule. He was a horse, but Halas left him pissed off, sky-high angry and in no frame of mind to excel the following day.

Bishop told me the club was just left in a funk. They were flat and easy pickings for the voracious Giants. On any given Sunday in the NFL, any team can win, but any damn team can also get blown out.

BUFFONE: Speaking of being in a funk, I've been watching this story involving the Bears fining and suspending Martellus Bennett for taking down Kyle Fuller. I don't know what the drill really is.

COPPOCK: TV timeout. Let me offer up an explanation. Several days into training camp (summer of '14), the Bears fined and suspended Martellus Bennett, a damn good tight end, after he was involved in a minor dust-up with DB Kyle Fuller, the club's top draft pick out of Virginia Tech. Of course, the hysterical Chicago media treated this whole shebang like it was Wounded Knee.

My God, you talk about drama queens. Most of the writers in town are in the Bears' hip pocket, so Bennett was being portrayed as a socio-political terrorist.

When I was very young, I do recall Halas telling the defense during a full-blown, two-hour workout, not to "bang the quarterback." The way he said it, I damn near keeled over I was laughing so hard.

The Old Man was a trip. But did you ever see Halas fine a guy or go haywire because of a fight in training camp?

BUFFONE: No. Never. Not once. The Old Man never said a thing when we had fights. The assistant coaches, especially Abe Gibron, loved 'em. They thought fights were great. We had the damn things every day.

So, what happened after the fight?

You took a shower, you cooled down, you apologized, and you went out to dinner. That was it. The NFL isn't supposed to be buddy-buddy. Guys are renegades. They aren't social workers who sit in a lotus position and whisper, "I want everyone to pretend you're a flower."

My ass.

Marc Trestman wanted everything to run smoothly, I guess.

COPPOCK: Here's the second half of this doubleheader.

Bennett dances to his own drum. He's a walking sound bite.

After the dust-up with Fuller, Bennett said, à la Allen Iverson, that this was practice and that shit happens. Plus, he basically mocked Trestman when he said, regarding a fine, "I can afford it, but I'm not sure what he'll fine me for."

Let's also mention this.

A classic group of guys: that's legendary broadcaster Jack Brickhouse second to left, right next to to Dick Butkus, and third from the right you have O.B., feeding me one-liners.

Trestman was so upset about the skirmish that he stopped practice with about 10 minutes left on the clock. This just screams overreaction. What coach does that?

BUFFONE: I gotta believe that we just don't know the whole story. You know I love Martellus Bennett, the player, but I don't like Bennett, the person. I don't like his "Black Unicorn" routine or the fact that he crawls back to the huddle. But he can flat-out play. He'll loaf on you every once in a while, but he is a player.

I think Trestman tried to develop a nice, cozy atmosphere. Go back to my day. Can you imagine Halas fining or suspending a guy like Mike Ditka or Bill George? Atkins would have told him to get lost. We were as cozy as a mongoose and a cobra. We were getting ready for a game that week, not chanting, "We are one in spirit."

We were building up intensity for Sunday, not roasting marshmallows at a campfire.

That's why we had very little rookie hazing when I joined the Bears. The veterans didn't give a shit about that stuff. They just wanted to know if a guy could play. I might have sung the Louisville Alma Mater at "rookie" night, but let me tell you another story about Halas.

After I played in the College All-Star Game, I drove down to Rensselaer to begin work with the Bears. I didn't so much as take a day off. When I get to camp, Halas saw me and asked me if I could sing, "Bear Down, Chicago Bears."

I told him, "I don't know the goddamn team fight song!"

I still don't know all the words after the first line.

COPPOCK: Join the crowd.

BUFFONE: The Old Man just looked at me and said, "Kid, learn it."

COPPOCK: Jeez, what a warm and engaging meet and greet. You land in north central Indiana and line up opposite Ditka twice a day for God's sake.

BUFFONE: The truth was that I was thrilled when the Bears peddled Mike to Philly after 1966. We were killing each other in practice.

Mike and I used to talk all the time about how we were just kicking the living crap out of each other and how, over the long haul, it wasn't going to help either one of us. We'd both bitch like crazy and then kill each other again the next day.

It was tough out there. Brutal. We both hurt like hell.

COPPOCK: Do you buy the old story that Halas really unloaded Ditka because he hit the roof when Mike described the Old Man's financial philosophy by saying Coach Halas "tosses around nickels like manhole covers?"

I don't.

That story will remain without closure. There has to be more to the story than Ditka popping off. Ditka could have been an All-Pro at seven positions: tight end, fullback, slot back, all three linebacker spots, and strong safety.

In the early '60s, there wasn't a more complete player in the NFL with the possible exception of Jimmy Brown.

And the Old Man got rid of Mike. Go figure.

My son Ryan, a fixture in aeronautics at Purdue University.

BUFFONE: Halas and Ditka. God they were so damn much alike. Both guys hated to lose. Both guys were beyond stubborn. To them, giving in and compromising was like a loss of manhood.

So, for the very reasons the Old Man traded Mike to the Eagles, those same reasons were why Halas brought him back to coach the Bears. When Halas looked at Ditka, in many regards, he really saw himself.

You know when the Bears drafted Mike out of Pitt that they really thought of him first as a linebacker and secondly as a tight end.

Listen, Halas loved tough guys, characters who played their guts out to win, and that's what Ditka was all about.

COPPOCK: Suppose Marc Trestman or (ex-Bears GM) Phil Emery had called you and said we want you to talk to our players about what Halas meant to pro football.

Would you have done it?

BUFFONE: Nope. It would be a waste of breath.

These guys don't know who Halas was and they really don't give a damn. You think they'd believe me if I said the Bears once played seven games in 10 days, traveling by train just to showcase the league and feature a guy by the name of Red Grange so that they could keep pro football alive?

They could care less.

Today's guys only care about money and how many years they're gonna play. If I talked to them, I'd be talking to a wall.

They would never believe that Halas got mad on Sunday and threw his coat at an official. Or about the time he kicked wide receiver Johnny Morris in the shins after he screwed up a pass pattern.

COPPOCK: Do you remember Halas just pounding lumps on Roger Leclerc, a guy who might just be the worst kicker the Bears have ever had?

God, Roger could be hopeless. The divots he used to kick up at Cubs Park were bigger than Phil Mickelson hitting a sand wedge from 60 yards out.

BUFFONE: This is right in my wheelhouse. I remember we lost a ballgame when Leclerc missed three makeable field goals. If he makes two out of three, we walk off a winner.

Halas just skinned him alive in the locker-room after the game. You know how Halas could bend words. He started calling Leclerc, a "cocksucker."

The old man was just livid. I mean out of his mind with anger. He ripped Roger to pieces. All Leclerc could do was just sit there and take it.

COPPOCK: That reminds me of Ditka's first game as head coach of the Bears, Opening Day in 1982. Billy Sims and the Lions beat a Bears team that really beat itself—I mean fuckin' beat itself.

Anyway, Dan Jiggetts, a great guy, just got caved in at left tackle by Bubba Baker, a ferocious pass rusher for the Lions. I remember three things about that postgame locker-room.

One, poor Dan was in tears. I think he figured he might get cut on the team plane. Baker just climbed into his jock.

Two, Ditka was so ticked that he told Mike Adamle and me that he might put the entire offensive line on waivers.

Three, Bob Avellini had something like seven face cuts. He was ripped to shreds. He looked like he'd been eaten by Hannibal Lecter. Pat McCaskey, the club's PR man at the time, told us not to point TV cameras at Bob, so naturally we all did.

Bob looked like he'd been French kissed with a meat cleaver.

And what am I thinking during all of this?

God, would this locker-room be a blast if Halas were here. You see, Mike was doing his best Halas impersonation.

BUFFONE: Back to Bennett and Fuller. If Halas were alive today and coaching, he wouldn't have said one damn word. People say, "Well, today's players are different," and they are in many respects, but they are still guys who are a little bit nuts. You have to be to play this game,

Think about Butkus.

He couldn't stand this defensive end we had named Marty Amsler. Marty was soft. Butkus just hated him. If Dick and Amsler would have slugged it out, Halas probably would have had to fight to suppress his laughter. That was the Old Man at practice. He loved tension.

And he will always be the Chicago Bears.

I loved the coach. I think I understood better than other guys what he had to do to make this league work and then he went out every week and did it. He was the toughest man I ever knew, other than my old man.

COPPOCK: The Bears are no longer the Monsters of the Midway. Hello, they've won just two world titles in 68 years. You know what they are?

An endless string of tough guys in the Halas mold, individually memorable but just not translating into great and sustaining teams.

Casares, George, Atkins, Eddie O'Bradovich, Wally Chambers, Doug Plank, Gary Fencik, Mike Singletary, Wilber Marshall, Otis Wilson, Jimbo Covert, Tom Thayer, Payton, Hampton, McMichael, Dent, Urlacher, Briggs, Tillman, and of course, that colorful Italian guy at linebacker named Buffone..

BUFFONE: Okay, I'll accept that. I gave a damn. That's why I love Hamp and Mongo so damn much. They were brutes. They pounded you physically and mentally.

They never let up.

You know, they were both really meant to play for Halas in leather helmets. That's the kind of competition that defined them. They were men who left everything they had on the field, whether it was at practice or game day.

You let the guys fight at practice. It gets them ready to kill someone on Sunday.

Guys like that rarely come around anymore. It's a shame.

chapter 29

The Sunshine Boys

COPPOCK: Buffone and O'Bradovich.

They are, of course, two aging and engaging warriors. Two guys who played a combined 24 years during an era when pro football wasn't as lightning quick as it is today but was, in its own way, significantly rougher.

Hell, when O'Bradovich joined the Bears in '62, the clothesline was still very much part of the game. But these two legends found themselves beloved by a whole new generation in their roles on the radio, tackling football issues and players who incur their wrath when they don't put out 100 percent on the field. Buff and O.B. didn't do it with helmets or pads anymore; they did it with a microphone.

They've been damn good at it too. Legitimate appointment radio—a cash cow for Mitch Rosen and WSCR-670 The Score.

BUFFONE: Let me tell ya why our show works. I didn't play trombone or tuba for 14 years; I played pro football. You can't bullshit me and you can't bullshit O.B.

What we do is completely spontaneous. No one knows what we're gonna say because we never know what we're gonna say!

COPPOCK: Buffone is talking about a great Windy City tradition, as much a part of Chi-Town as crooked pols, hot dogs overloaded with mustard, Italian beef falling off a bun, and pizza thick enough to satiate a Great Dane.

Doug is more than justifiably proud of "Doug and O.B. Post Game," a show that has run on The Score for nearly a generation. The show, following every Bears game, is simply must-listen radio for anybody who sweats blood worrying about the Blue and Orange. If you know either guy, you know this is just too easy; the show's audience surges whenever the Bears get left on the wrong side of the score, especially if the Bears get roasted.

Rosen, a solid radio man and the station's longtime program director, earned his bones back in the '80s producing late-night talk-show king "Chicago" Eddie Schwartz. Mitch, a stand-up guy, will tell you straight up, "It's interesting to note that when the Bears lose, ratings and interest are higher."

It's due to the completely honest opinions these guys bring to the table.

ED O'BRADOVICH: You know sometimes we confront each other while the game is going on. I mean, we scream at each other. But we know there's a strong degree of mutual respect.

We never have meetings to set up the shows. We are as live as the game itself.

When we were first approached about doing the show, meetings were discussed, but I told them, "I will not go to one pre-show meeting—not now, not ever."

COPPOCK: On a rainy summer morning in 2014, Big Ed, the pride and joy of Proviso East High School, arrived at Buffone's fashionable residence on the edge of Chicago's trendy Little Italy neighborhood. The home, which Doug shares with his pixie-cute wife, Dana, and their kids, is beautifully furnished. Not garish. No art deco. The place has a very simple degree of understated class.

Eddie and Doug had been asked to hop in the saddle to discuss the legacies of Dick Butkus and Gale Sayers with a crew from NFL Films.

I was there to chat with them for this book and to watch a pair of longtime buddies raise some hell.

Both guys waxed poetic, as they tossed out one-liners, anecdotes, and stories about two of the most majestic athletes in pro football history, the Beauty and the Butkus.

Frankly, the toughest part of their day was getting from the lower level of Chez Buffone up to the second floor.

O'BRADOVICH: I could never live in a place like this. I love it, but with those damn stairs, my knees wouldn't last a week.

COPPOCK: Buffone admitted that the stairs don't grant him any favors either. There are no complaints. Both guys understand the price they paid to play the game they love.

O.B., always something of a peacock, arrived for the taping in a gorgeous white on white dress shirt with Ivy League buttons offset by classy gray slacks.

Buffone, who's favorite word has to be "casual," was wearing a red pullover.

O.B.'s hair is Colonel Sanders white, while Doug's is western Pennsylvania gray.

Your imagination wanders and you think yes, this must be how Doug's old man looked in his early seventies—rugged, steel-tough.

The guy directing the two stalwarts basically had a day off. All he had to do was toss out a line and O.B. and Doug ran like hell with it. Honest to God, they practically went non-stop, each guy playing off the other in remarkably fluid fashion.

Like Carson and McMahon or Mick and Keith. Except, they're both Jackie Gleason's Ralph Kramden—cantankerous, brawling, tough, and irascible, with a presence as pronounced as the long-gone Chicago stockyards behind the old International Amphitheater over at 42nd and Halsted.

Buffone and O'Bradovich.

Get the hell out of their way. They're still knocking down opponents.

During a break in the action, I hit one of Buffone's hot buttons. I talked to him about the 2010 NFC Championship Game, the so-called "Cutler game," won by Green Bay over the Bears 21–14 at Soldier Field.

Losing that game cost the Bears a Super Bowl ticket.

BUFFONE: I got nauseated as I listened to all of those so-called experts who tweeted that Cutler was a quitter because he waved off early in the second half with his knee problem. Take Deion Sanders, for example. Here's a guy

Two first-class, stand-up guys: WSCR program director Mitch Rosen and the incomparable Ed O'Bradovich.

who had, maybe, one tackle in about 52 games, saying Cutler didn't have any heart.

No heart, my ass. Cutler has balls. He's got brass.

Honestly, I didn't like Mike Ditka saying he would have had to be paralyzed before he left a game that important. Hey, I was a linebacker. I probably would have stayed in. I could still engage people. Even with a bad wheel, I could still chase down a play on the weak side. But Cutler with the shaky knee couldn't plant, so he couldn't throw.

The coaches didn't do him any favors either.

Who's Cutler supposed to be? God?

COPPOCK: Maybe the Bears didn't do Jay any favors when they announced over the press box P.A. system after Cutler left the ballgame that his status was "questionable." They should have taken the heat off the kid by saying, "Wave good bye, Jay is headed to Northwestern Hospital."

BUFFONE: We get far more intelligent callers than other postgame shows, but we also get people who are clueless.

I remember a few years ago, some lady called in after the Bears got trounced and said, "Doug, you aren't being fair to the team. They'll improve next week and really get better as the year goes on."

My hair was standing on end I was so damn mad. Everyone knew the Bears were playing like crap and now I've got Mother Teresa on the phone.

So I leveled with this girl. "Lady, you're a loser. You are really a loser. I don't know if you even know a football from a foot stool." But I called her what I thought she was—a loser.

COPPOCK: At that point, if you still haven't seen why pre-show meetings for O.B. and Doug are fruitless, just skip to the next chapter.

Yes, the Doug and O.B. show works because the two guys played the game nearly a quarter century combined and they're not shy about sharing their passion about it. O.B. has a championship from '63. (Buffone can't hide, nor does he try to, his envy of Ed having the symbol of pro football excellence.)

But students, keep this in mind. The ex-Bear routine would last about eight minutes if the audience sensed that they were just a couple of housemen pulling heavy duty for the Halas Hall public relations machine.

These guys are still so religiously devoted to the Bears that they take every blunder by the club as a personal affront. Honestly, if the Bears lose the coin toss, both guys want to throw a challenge flag.

Not to mention, Buff and O.B. have become a revenue bonanza for the Score.

There is no way you can downplay the value the station has enjoyed by having these two erstwhile legends on the payroll. Rival stations have tried various combos against Doug and Ed and absolutely gone nowhere fast.

As big as the old pros are on Sundays, having them available as prime-time contributors during the week may be where their true value really lies.

BUFFONE: We've blasted a lot of athletes over the years. I remember one guy we just nailed was Marion Barber, the kid the Bears picked up from Dallas. Do you remember the clueless blunder that guy came up with against Denver a few years ago? I remember it was 2011.

It was absolute football stupidity.

The Bears were trying to protect a lead and all the son of a bitch had to do was keep the clock running and we win. Instead, the jerk runs out of bounds.

I thought my head was going to fly off.

You know the rest of the story. Tim Tebow and the Broncos had time to kick a field goal, force overtime, and then win in the extra period. Lovie Smith should have made that idiot Barber walk back to Chicago.

The only thing good about Barber was that he wasn't Chester Taylor. On his best days, Taylor couldn't play dead.

COPPOCK: There's a cruel irony here. Barber rushed for 108 yards versus the Broncos and scored a touchdown on a nine-yard dash.

Then, of course, he suffered the mother of all brain cramps when he failed to get in the fetal position and stay inbounds. I'll always believe that if Jim Finks had been the Bears GM at the time, he would have cut Barber within 24 hours just to make a point.

O'BRADOVICH: I never know what Doug's gonna say and he never knows what I'm gonna say once the show goes on.

Rants are a great way to break the sound barrier of life.

BUFFONE: People will ask me if I'm ever going to retire or maybe walk away from the show when I'm 75.

Why the hell would I do that?

I love the damn thing and I love our audience.

COPPOCK: This is going to shock a helluva of a lot of people, most notably Dan Bernstein.

I'm not in love with Dan Bernstein's act, or for that reason, Bernstein the person, but the fact is I have a great deal of respect for his on-air persona. The Score's afternoon drive host actually does a lot of thing that I've done over the years in Indy, Chicago, and New York. He plays the role of the Peck's Bad Boy. He is the closest thing Chicago sports talk radio has to a man you love to hate. Believe me, that isn't all bad. It's actually terrific.

So he treats his listeners like dirt. What's the big deal? Those callers are getting their 11 seconds of fame when Bernstein tells them to buzz off.

He leads with his chin. He begs you to smack him. Bernstein's a study in grade-A defiance. When he calls his listeners idiots he's no different than a classic wrestling heel taunting the crowd.

Really, in a different lifetime, Bernstein could have been Bobby Heenan managing the Iron Sheik. I can easily see him with platinum blonde hair and a sparkling, sequined top with the word "Bernsy" on the back screaming at Jesse "the Body" Ventura about an upcoming "Loser Leaves Town Match" in Pittsburgh or Terre Haute.

To do what Bernstein does takes stones. You have to accept the fact that a lot of people are going to go out of their way to make your life miserable. Dan has shown for years that he can handle the abuse. God know he thrives on it.

BUFFONE: Let me tell you about an episode with Bernstein that landed me in the principal's office. Dan and I were doing a cross-talk thing on the air when he got on my nerves. You know Bernsy likes to push the envelope as much as possible.

I was getting pissed off, I mean big-time pissed. I told him to lay off. So what does Bernstein say? How about this? He tells me to keep quiet because I'm too old to go after him. Too old to go after him—I could have murdered the son of a bitch.

You know I've got a temper. So after Dan had gotten completely under my skin, I grabbed him. But this wasn't a gentle grab. I got him on the floor and began to choke him. Christ, he was turning purple. Fortunately, some guys in the control room came in and pulled me off him.

I really felt bad when it was over. I mean really bad. I knew I could have seriously hurt him.

Now, here's the punch line. A month or so later, a listener called in and said he was disappointed in me for how I handled the Bernstein situation.

So, you're thinking this guy was taking me to task, right? No way. This listener says he wishes O.B. would have jumped him because Ed would have *killed* him.

He was probably right. Fortunately, Dan and I extended the olive branch.

COPPOCK: When O.B. and Doug resumed with NFL Films, they continued to mix sincerity with hilarity. There were times when they both just doubled up laughing about a long-gone memory and there were also times when they turned very serious.

BUFFONE: You know the Bears never had any racial trouble when I was there, but it was still a very turbulent time. Brian Piccolo and Gale Sayers were the first teammates of opposite races to room together. When it took place, Gale stood up unannounced and told us, "I'm a Chicago Bear, first and then I'm an African American."

The gesture had an effect on all of us.

Because, as you know, Sayers was a proud man.

COPPOCK: O'Bradovich tossed in a zinger at his tag team partner and friend.

O'BRADOVICH (TO DOUG): I had a speaking part in *Brian's Song.* Did you? Go on. Admit it. I had a speaking part. You got shut out.

BUFFONE: Yeah, you should have won a fuckin' Emmy.

COPPOCK: By now, the two pals, whose friendship dates nearly a half-century, have the director, cameraman, and sound operator howling with laughter.

Doug and O.B. They bust all the radio rules and laugh like hell while doing it.

Is there such a thing as 70-year-old Peck's Bad Boys?

Just stay out of their way.

BUFFONE: Here's a subject. Let me tell you about John Brockington, the former Packer. He was one tough hombre, who never got the big-time credit he deserved.

COPPOCK: FYI, who was the first NFL back to rush for 1,000 yard in each of his first three seasons? Answer: John Brockington. The guy was a classic north-south runner.

BUFFONE: My point exactly. I always felt all the people—like the people up in Green Bay—were so wrapped up in the greatness of Paul Hornung and Jimmy Taylor that they never really understood just how good John was.

I can tell you why this guy had a short career (seven years). Green Bay just drove Brock into the ground. They wore the kid out.

COPPOCK: It's really a shame. The guy should have gone to the Hall of Fame. He was an All-Pro in each of his first three seasons. Once the Pack traded MacArthur Lane, Brockington carried the Green Bay offense.

BUFFONE: I hit John one time and I really saw stars. I heard birds chirping; I mean I was lost. We hit each other helmet to helmet. We just crashed like freight trains, just like my collision with Eddie Marinaro.

I was knocked out.

I only missed a few plays. I was lucky. It was a case where we both sold out. I've got all the respect in the world for that guy and I think he probably respected me as well.

He wasn't like that prick, Monty Stickles, who played for the 49ers and Saints. That bastard was a psycho. I saw him get ejected once for running into an official. I mean, who the hell does that?

We went down to play New Orleans one time and Joe Fortunato, a really underrated linebacker, was giving me the rundown on Stickles.

Joe told me to keep my eyes on this guy for obvious reasons. Now, to play football, you have to live in a state of denial. You simply can't believe that you're going to get hurt, but you also have to know your surroundings, keep your eyes open, look around, and watch your back.

So we're playing Stickles and New Orleans and I mean this guy didn't want to just hurt other players, he wanted to end their day. He was always looking to crack back, take a guy's knees out. He'd try and cut block you to death. He was always after your knees. You know what I did?

I took it to him. I hit him again and again. I wanted him to know how it felt to hurt. I just did it cleanly. Made me smile.

The last thing I wanted to do was shake the bastard's hand after the ballgame.

COPPOCK: The final gun.

Closure.

The game was over, but in fact the chapter was still ongoing, right?

BUFFONE: When I got to the locker-room, I sat back and took a long drag on a Marlboro. Then the thought process began. You started thinking and rethinking about being on that field for 75 plays.

Reliving that game. You don't have any idea how draining it was.

You were mentally exhausted and your body hurt like hell. If you're seriously hurt, you knew it. But there were plenty of times you don't know how badly banged up you were until the next day.

COPPOCK: That sounds like Dan Hampton when he played for the Bears. When a game ended, he went straight to the training room to have his knees worked on and then came back to sit by his locker.

Just sat there.

He was slowly coming back to reality.

Hamp was always great with the press, but you had to wait for his body language to stop saying, "Don't even think about coming over to me with one of your idiotic questions," before you approached the big guy.

He had to personally exhale from the pain and exhaustion of the war he had fought on the field. Fans had no idea how scary that was. McMichael was the same way. Watching Mongo remove his knee wraps was beyond painful. You could see the guy was enduring pain that a normal person could never endure.

BUFFONE: I can relate to that.

You know, I've never figured this out, but I used to feel chills after games. All the time. I'd actually get the shakes. I thought at times, "Shit, am I going to die?"

To this day, I have no idea what my body was doing.

COPPOCK: I think it was telling you, "Back off, I can't take any more of this crap, at least not today."

BUFFONE: Think about that. I'd get the shakes. I know it was either from nicotine or the intensity of being out on that field like a madman.

Maybe I'll never know. I do know this—it was a son of a bitch. The first few hours after a game are just as tough as the actual game itself. The game was never over. That's the whole point.

The damn game was never over, especially when you lost.

Then came Tuesday. That's when you broke down game tape with the coaches. You've heard the old football saying, "The eye in the sky doesn't lie?"

It doesn't.

If you messed up, it's right there for everybody to see. If you made a mistake, the coaches screamed, "Rewind!"

You looked for the nearest desk to hide under. You heard the clicking sound of doom and maybe you looked at the damn play several times. Humiliation 101.

You wanted to shout, "Look, I know what I was supposed to do when we ran the 56-over defense. I know the weak-side tackle shifted to the nose guard spot. I know I have to engage the tight end if he blocked down. I know I've got to be ready for the strong-side offensive tackle and a pulling guard. *I KNOW!*"

I mean, there were legs and elbows and jock straps flying all over the place. I got that. I knew I couldn't allow myself to get "hooked"—couldn't let anybody block me on my inside shoulder or the gap would be opened as wide as the Red Sea.

I knew all that.

But coaches were paid to ram things down your throat, like elementary teachers with megalomania. Over and over and over again, they never shut up.

You had one salvation. There was no pressure on you when they showed the film because everybody was gonna get called out.

That's just the way it was. Hell, I got belted so many times out there. It's one thing to hit the brick wall, it's quite another when the damn thing hits back.

Do you remember that little round guy who played for the Colts and Miami?

COPPOCK: Sure, Don Nottingham, the Human Bowling Ball. He was built like a fire hydrant. If you hit him high, you'd wind up in the 10th row.

BUFFONE: One time, Don just ran right over me. I mean, the little shit just totaled me. I was lying on my ass after it happened.

So, when we're going over the play on film, guys are laughing like hell about the Bowling Ball getting the best of me. I laughed along with them. Then the coaches turned on another guy and ran his play.

One way or another, everybody got called out.

COPPOCK: Did we leave out anything regarding vomiting?

BUFFONE: Yeah, you're gonna love this. It's a true story.

We were playing the Giants in the Jersey Meadowlands and my parents came in to watch the game with some of their friends. As I said, I used to call them the Hillbillies. My old man didn't really care all that much about football, but my mom was just rabid about the game.

The night before the game, I got together with them to have dinner. Ma had made a ton of pasta and sausage. I ate like it was my last meal on earth. I mean, I had enough marinara sauce to blanket Italy.

So, the next day, our defense was introduced and as I ran through the goal posts, I vomited. I mean, I hurled.

Hell, I was throwing up all afternoon. My stomach was a trampoline. The guys in the huddle all thought I'd gotten smashed the night before.

Of course, I never said a word to my mom.

I didn't want to hurt her feelings.

chapter 30

Buffone's Top 10 Most Competitive Bears

COPPOCK: Welcome to "Buffone Airlines" Flight 55.

Destination?

The Land of the 10 most competitive Bears over the past 50 years.

Fasten your seatbelt.

Your captain on this flight will be the 14-year-veteran linebacker, along with first officer Chet Coppock. You know me. I'm the loud mouth whose frequent babbling has left people in a stupor for years.

Of course, there will be no meals in coach class. This is 2015, for heaven's sake. You're downright lucky that we'll let you people spend five bucks to buy a bag of stale peanuts.

Feel free to boo, jeer, cheer, and tell Doug to seek psychiatric care whenever you damn well feel like it.

For fun, why don't you, as a reader, jot down your list and see how it compares.

Take it away, Mr. B.

BUFFONE: There was always blood, chinstraps, and even a helmet or two on the field after many a play with these guys. Here is my list.

10. Jimbo Covert (LT). It's a crime, a damn crime, that he's not in the Pro Football Hall of Fame. The guy deserves the yellow blazer. The only guy in his league in the '80s was Anthony Munoz.

9. Steve "Mongo" McMichael (DT). A legitimate throwback who recorded 95 sacks playing inside and had to have at least 200 pressures. Any guy with a rattlesnake tattooed on his leg is my kind of player.

COPPOCK: Hey, Buffone, I hate to bust up your flow, but I need to mention this. Mongo never uses the passive when the active is available. I used to love to emcee Bears luncheons where he was the main attraction.

God, he cursed like a longshoreman.

But you know what was funny? Women just loved the guy's act. He was and always will be a classically endearing bad boy.

Okay, back to work.

BUFFONE: Jeez, thank God you only took up seven lines. Generally, Coppock, you can't say your name in less than 10 paragraphs. If you had given the Gettysburg Address, it would have been the original manuscript for *War and Peace.*

8. Brian Urlacher (MLB). The first time I saw the kid, he was playing the Sam. I said that's nuts, he's got to play the middle. Phenomenal speed, great attitude, a Hall of Fame lock.

If Lovie and his gang of misfits would have given him an offense, he would have played in three Super Bowls.

7. Doug Atkins (DE). The guy was frightening. Doug had that very soft Tennessee drawl, which belied the rage he brought to the ballpark. The guy was a terror. His battles with Jim Parker, the old Baltimore Colts tackle, were epic.

COPPOCK: You forgot to mention that Doug established records for complaints about the offense that will never be touched. You know the guy had the ability to leapfrog tackles.

I mean, who does that?

Nobody.

But keep this in mind. Big Doug was a Southeastern high-jump champ during his days at Tennessee.

BUFFONE: Next up:

6. Bill George (MLB). The Greek. I really would have killed to have played with him. The vets I joined when I hooked up with the Bears in '66 spoke with such reverence for Bill. George was like God to them. He was a Pro Bowl fixture. George was responsible for the phrase "Red Dog" being used to talk about linebackers who could rush the passer. This is a fact. Players on other teams dreaded having to play against Bill George.

5. Ed O'Bradodvich (DE). O.B. was funny as hell, but he was absolutely relentless.

The guy had a mean streak that was a mile long. Losing just tore him up. He wanted to win as badly as any guy I ever played with. A quarterback killer.

COPPOCK: Timeout, Commander.

The gentleman nicknamed O.B., seated in 1-A, would like to throw in his two dollar's worth.

O'BRADOVICH: It just kills me that Doug Buffone didn't get more pub during his career. He would have started for every team in the league in every one of his 14 seasons. I mean, he would have been a starter with the Pittsburgh and Dallas Super Bowl teams.

Buffone was that good.

He just played on so many lousy clubs that never got anywhere near .500. If you would have put him behind the (the Vikings) Purple People Eaters or the (Los Angeles Rams) Fearsome Foursome, his stats would have been phenomenal.

He was elite.

Doug was the most underrated player of my era.

COPPOCK: O.B., I know guys are going to say that you're building up Buffone because you tag-team with him on WSCR Radio. But let me add this: How many people know that one year before sacks were recorded, Doug had 18 QB traps?

Laughing it up with two guys who always played "George Halas" tough: Steve McMichael and Dan Hampton.

BUFFONE: Hey, the fact is, I'll always wonder just how good I could have been if I'd played with the Steelers with Mean Joe Greene, L.C. Greenwood, and Ernie Holmes.

You can bet the flippin' rent I would have gone to my share of Pro Bowls.

4. Walter Payton (RB). He had such remarkable endurance. I don't know where he got it.

Do you even remember the guy running out of bounds? He was everything that Franco Harris wasn't.

Guys played like hell for Payton because they knew he was putting his body on the line every Sunday.

3. Gale Sayers (RB). I can see the eyebrows out there raising already. But here's what people really didn't see when it came to Gale. He was not just an elegant runner; the guy could flat-out block.

Plus, he was a great pass receiver coming out of the backfield.

And he returned punts and kickoffs. Christ, one year, he led the league in kickoffs with 37 yards a return. Those are reckless positions on a football field—coming across the middle, returning punts and kickoffs—not for the faint-hearted players, believe me.

Anybody who doesn't think Gale was a competitor doesn't know what football's all about.

2. Dan Hampton (DE/DT). I knew the first day I saw him that he was gonna own the NFL. God, the big fella was just a tremendous football player. You could sense that his presence just made 10 other players that much better. Plus, he never took a play off. Anybody who saw Hampton saw the real deal.

He laughed about playing hurt. The game meant everything to him. He truly honored the business. I'll always have this feeling that I was like a big brother to him.

1. Dick Butkus (MLB). Who else do you put at No. 1?

The guy's the greatest football player in NFL history.

I've said this before, but it's criminal that he never got to play on a club that went to the playoffs.

COPPOCK: Okay, are you done?

I see two notable omissions.

Where are the bulging eyes of Mike Singletary? I know he played behind Hamp and Mongo, but tell me any Hall of Fame linebacker that didn't have help up front.

Round two: Wilber Marshall.

In the mid-'80s, he was the best pure defensive player in the game, a notch above Lawrence Taylor. He had one small weakness—he wasn't real strong dropping into coverage.

His personality was that of a quiet assassin.

Do you remember the belt he put on Joe Ferguson's sternum at the Pontiac Silverdome?

Ferguson, the Lions' quarterback, was left about three feet under the carpet. Ditka told me he thought Joe was dead.

BUFFONE: On behalf of Buffone Airlines, I'd like to thank you for flying with us today. It's been real, man.

chapter 31

Close Encounters of the Third Kind

COPPOCK: I have a feeling you are about to tell me something here that will raise some eyebrows.

BUFFONE: Well, I had an "out of this world" encounter.

COPPOCK: I've never had a legitimate reason to question your sanity. So, when you tell me something in that warm, but politely firm tone of voice, I'm not going to just say, "No way" or "Jeez, did you start drinkin' again?"

BUFFONE: You wanna hear the story?

COPPOCK: Sounds out of this world.

BUFFONE: (Chomping on his ever-present cigar) When I was a young kid, maybe 13 to 14 years old, my mom sent me out to get some sugar from one of our neighbors. I had to go through a woodsy area to get from our house to where the neighbor lived.

All of our company houses were separated by trees, bushes, and all kinds of foliage. On my way back, I know this sounds crazy, but I saw something....

COPPOCK: What?

BUFFONE: I saw an alien.

COPPOCK: (Speechless) Hello?

BUFFONE: I swear to God.

COPPOCK: What gives?

BUFFONE: It had this incredible aura, an almost blinding glow.

I ran like hell and hid my ass under an embankment, but I know there were people, some kind of people, that got off that thing—whatever it was—and they saw me.

COPPOCK: They got off a thing…you mean a spaceship?

BUFFONE: Yeah, that was it. They looked right at me.

COPPOCK: Were they friendly? Did they smile?

BUFFONE: Hell no, they were aliens.

COPPOCK: Were they hostile, menacing, glaring, curious…?

BUFFONE: Aliens.

COPPOCK: What did they look like?

BUFFONE: If Al Sharpton and Chelsea Clinton had a kid.

COPPOCK: My God!

BUFFONE: I know what I saw, and what I saw was real. Then I got the hell out of there.

COPPOCK: What did you tell your parents when you got home?

BUFFONE: I didn't tell them a damn thing. What the hell was I gonna say? They would have thought I was a nut job.

I firmly believe and will always believe that what I saw was real. Actually, my mom was pissed because I had to tell her that I had spilled the sugar.

COPPOCK: Okay, let me play reporter now....

You were raised in a very small community. Your family had to struggle from day to day, week to week. So forgive me for suggesting that on one night, a young kid, an honor roll student with an active mind, just sort of went out of body for a couple of minutes?

BUFFONE: Not exactly, but, here's something that will back up what I saw. At the time, there had been alien sightings all over western Pennsylvania. A lot of people said they saw aliens. All around us was like alien central. It's like the loony space creeps decided our geography was their new Eden or something.

Go figure.

I actually had another experience that was similar to the first one, if not stronger and even more realistic.

COPPOCK: So you were in the throes of what would be known as "the Alien Era?"

BUFFONE: Yeah, something like that.

After I saw that first alien arrival, my pal John Kulick and I began to go hunting for aliens.

COPPOCK: Hunting for aliens? Whatever happened to baseball on radio?

BUFFONE: We wanted to flush out the little suckers.

COPPOCK: See any?

BUFFONE: We came across another ship. It just rose up from the dirty water of the Allegheny River. This time, the ship was shaped like a cigar, but it had the same kind of glow.

And just like the first time, there were people or aliens that looked right at John and me. I was driving my old man's '49 Chrysler when I saw this thing.

COPPOCK: And?

BUFFONE: And nothing. We just stared each other down. We let those alien punks know who ran the show.

COPPOCK: Okay, Patrick Henry, thanks for defending Earth. What happened after you put the fear of God into them?

BUFFONE: Then, John and I went home.

We felt good. We had saved the planet.

COPPOCK: It was time to tell Sam.

BUFFONE: There was no way I was gonna tell my old man. He would have beaten the shit out of me. The old man was living in the mines. You think he's gonna buy me talking about aliens for Christ's sake?

COPPOCK: No more aliens after that?

BUFFONE: Not a sign, not a word. Later that summer, I also went out in search of Bigfoot.

No kidding, John and I would go out every night because we thought we had seen something gigantic in the woods. It was probably a bear, but we were crazy enough to think it just had to be Bigfoot.

COPPOCK: Did the ET feel dangerous, evil, peaceful, what?

BUFFONE: Just an alien feeling.

COPPOCK: What in the hell is an alien feeling?

BUFFONE: Hi, alien, how are you?

COPPOCK: I have no words here.

BUFFONE: (Laughing) Jeez, that's a first!

Several seconds of silence pass by. Coppock gives a history lesson.

COPPOCK: In 1947, Mac Brazel, a local farmer in New Mexico, discovered unidentified debris in a cow pasture about 75 miles from Roswell. The Feds wasted little time before declaring that the flying saucer that some people claimed to have seen was simply a hot air balloon.

What else were they going to say, so help me President Harry Truman?

And despite statements from the U.S. government that it was simply conducting an experiment, Roswell became a town of legend.

Matters weren't helped much in the 1950s when the Air Force supposedly conducted additional experiments that featured the unloading of crash test dummies that looked one helluva lot like you might figure the average alien would look like.

So, Buffone, grab the mic. You saw aliens on two different occasions, but no words were spoken and there was no confrontation of any kind?

BUFFONE: Yeah.

COPPOCK: Roswell still draws its share of people annually who believe with every bone in their body, that yes, there was some kind of UFO that landed in the cow pasture and that others have followed.

You believe you saw aliens and a space ship.

BUFFONE: I did see them, yeah.

COPPOCK: Maybe it was a couple of guys out in the woods playing pranks?

BUFFONE: No.

COPPOCK: Were you drinking?

BUFFONE: I was 13.

COPPOCK: Hallucinating?

BUFFONE: Nope.

COPPOCK: You're sure?

BUFFONE: I saw what I saw, and I saw an alien.

COPPOCK: That's your story and you're sticking to it?

BUFFONE: Yep.

COPPOCK: I believe you, I guess.

BUFFONE: Damn right. I shoulda got a medal or something.

COPPOCK: Why?

BUFFONE: We could have all been evaporated had I not stared them down.

COPPOCK: We're done here with the alien thing, Doug.

chapter 32

The Last Hurrah... Buffone Reflects

COPPOCK: The Coppock-Buffone lunch tour arrives near the tail end of February 2015 at Chicago's plush East Bank Club, arguably the most famous workout facility between the two coasts.

Their blueberry muffins are the stuff of legend. Michael Jordan and Oprah are both members. Madonna, Bruce Springsteen, Tony Bennett, and Robert De Niro have all walked through the club's doors.

As we walk into the place, my thoughts go back 30-plus years to the early '80s, when Doug, just a few years out of football, used to savagely pound the heavy bag adjacent to the quarter-mile indoor track on the club's third level.

At the time, shortly after the arrival of Reagan and MTV, I had always felt that No. 55 was still unleashing the remnants of the aggression he brought to the gridiron after 22 years of competitive football through high school, Louisville, and his remarkable 14-year run with the Bears. The sweat would slide off Doug's nose, while his hair would toss off beads of perspiration as he hammered the bag seemingly non-stop.

However, it's a much different day for Buffone. He admitted that he hadn't been to EBC in years, but what is really on his mind is life—where he's been, where he is now, and where he's going.

This is Doug's chapter. This is a man who sees the reality of the finish line.

BUFFONE: The ultimate reality of pro football doesn't really settle in until you've been away from the game for a while.

I'm 70 years old.

I hear all these stories about post-concussion syndrome and brain trauma and naturally, I begin to worry.

Hell yes, I worry. I don't wanna become a burden for Dana and my kids. I just hope to God I die in my sleep.

COPPOCK: Best way to go.

The team: Dana; my twins, Hailey and Heather; and my son Ryan.

BUFFONE: Absolutely. I did learn in my final years with the Bears that there just wasn't room for loyalty. Players want to believe there is, but there just isn't.

In my final year, I knew there were plays on the weak side I couldn't make anymore. The club could care less if you're old or young. All they know is that you screwed up. This is a game based on your performance on Sunday.

If it suffers, you aren't valuable to them anymore.

COPPOCK: While onlookers peer over at Doug, I began to think about the magnetism of a young Gale Sayers and just how pathetic it was watching the vaunted Kansas Comet in a worthless struggle, trying to find a new life with a shattered knee during his final year with the Bears in 1971.

Sayers was a very bright man who knew the game, and he wanted to be an NFL GM in the worst way. He paid his dues, but the league he had served with such remarkable physical grace wouldn't give him the time of day.

The NFL turned its back on Sayers the would-be executive, and frankly, I don't think Gale has ever forgiven the old guard for leaving him in the back of the bus.

BUFFONE: I never really talked to Gale about what he was going through.

You know he could be a very private guy.

But I knew the knee was killing him. Forget about running the ball, Gale struggled to even limp effectively. You knew the guy was crushed physically and worse than that, he was suffering emotionally. There were too damn many days at practice when Gale was limping so badly you wondered why the club had him in a uniform.

COPPOCK: The incomparable Sayers required just 68 games to grab his ticket to the Pro Football Hall of Fame.

Christ, he was All-Pro in his first five seasons.

That just amazed me. You know Hub Arkush, a guy who doesn't know half the football he thinks he knows, once had the gall to tell me he thought Sayers was overrated. What the hell? That's like saying the Sistine Chapel is overrated.

In '69, Sayers was named the NFL Comeback Player of the Year on a pathetic Bears team that went 1–13. The Bears were so damn bad in '69 I would have made them a 7-point 'dog versus Appalachian State.

During his last two seasons, he carried the ball a grand total of 36 times, including 13 carries in '71 for just 38 yards.

Game, set, and match, over and out.

BUFFONE: I'm pissed about Gale and Butkus. They never played in a postseason game. The Bears surrounded them with crap. Nothing but crap.

A 22-year-old kid is gonna run you over. You got young guys all over the field who wanna bust you up to build up their own stock.

People forget this, but Joe Namath played the last game of his career in Chicago. Joe and I got together at the old BBC, my place over on Division Street, the night before the game.

He was with the Rams.

Joe's knees, both of 'em, were just shot to hell. He had no business being on a football field, but Namath was tough. I know that "Broadway Joe" stuff had made a lot of people think he was all sizzle and no steak.

That's just crap.

Namath came out of the same region of Pennsylvania as me. He was from Beaver Falls. We grew up about an hour away from each other.

COPPOCK: I remember that game like it happened last Tuesday. I was doing public address for the Bears. It was back in October 1977, a Monday nighter in a heavy rain at Soldier Field.

Namath looked so strange wearing the Rams' Blue and Gold. He was so associated with the Jets' Green and White. For the record, Joe finished 16 of 40 with four interceptions. One of those picks was made by a distinguished gentleman named Doug Buffone.

The Bears were all over Namath.

The poor guy didn't have the wheels to get set in the pocket. The sizzling, hot release was still there, but he was playing on what had to be the knees of a 70-year-old man. He had to throw a dozen passes off his back foot.

Joe was done. His body was finished. He never laced on the pads again.

BUFFONE: Namath was probably thinking the same thing I was thinking after I retired from the game in '79.

I could have played on, but I could only go once every four weeks. I could have played till I was 50 under those scheduled circumstances.

I saw Johnny Unitas at San Diego when he was on the decline. It was just like Namath. Unitas may have been the greatest quarterback in NFL history, but when he left the Colts, he was history, washed up.

He was no longer Johnny Unitas.

This league is not primarily about sports or heroes or even legends. It is a business.

I always said that the Kenny Rogers song "The Gambler" was spot on: "You gotta know when to hold 'em...know when to fold 'em."

That's really what a career in the NFL is all about.

What was Halas thinking about in the early '70s when we were getting our asses handed to us every Sunday?

I've often wondered if the Old Man ever thought to himself, "Ya know, maybe the game has passed me by?"

COPPOCK: You know I just adored the Old Man. He'll always be my ultimate sports hero. I feel blessed that I had so many opportunities as a kid and as a young reporter to be around the coach.

But I'll never forget something Ralph Kurek, a durable running back out of Wisconsin who played for the Bears, told me about Halas.

Ralph, who became a successful advertising man, said to me years ago that he didn't think the Old Man really cared how lousy the ballclub was back in the early '70s.

Kurek offered this up for debate: "You know a lot of Halas' old buddies would gather around him and tell him, 'Ya know, Coach, things would be so much different if you were still on the sidelines. These guys today don't know how to motivate players. They just don't have what you had.'"

Now, Halas, the coach, was a raging pit bull after losses, but how much do we really know about Halas, the owner, during the Bears lean years back in the late '60s and '70s?

Maybe the Papa Bear was so damn stubborn because he just didn't want anybody to occupy his spot on the throne. That makes me wonder if he knew back in the early '60s that George Allen was the best coaching prospect in the NFL.

The Old Man could have made a very natural handoff to Allen after the Bears won the bundle in '63, but he didn't.

Was Halas, a guy who built the Bears and the league into a billion dollar industry, worried that Allen would step in, succeed big time, and make people forget about his legacy?

God, we could argue that question for a millennium.

BUFFONE: The more I think about age and the people around me, the more I wonder just where the hell the time went.

I used to color my hair all the time, but one day, I just said screw it. "I am what I am."

I would love to live to be 90, but I have to accept that I'm in the stretch run.

It's funny, when I got to Chicago, I looked at guys like Sid Luckman and said, "Gosh, they look old."

Now the young guys look at me and probably think I'm a fossil. That's me, eating leaves off the treetops, and waiting to be extinct.

That's just the way it works.

Hell yes, I wish I could suit up one more time and play a ballgame at Lambeau Field. But it's just not going to happen. You have to accept that and I like to believe I have.

Look at how big Johnny Carson was when he finally walked off *The Tonight Show.* Are you gonna tell me there weren't nights after Carson left that he didn't think to himself, "Maybe I retired too early?"

COPPOCK: Buffone's NFL pension pays him about $85,000 a year. That isn't chump change, but it seems woefully inadequate for a guy who subjected his body to 14 years of NFL abuse. I'm going to suggest that $140,000 per year would be a great deal more logical.

A Buffone family tradition: hunting with my son Doug Jr. in my hometown of Yatesboro, PA.

Hey, don't start screaming about me running a "Tag Day" for Doug Buffone.

The guy's had his financial ups and downs like virtually everybody else, but Buffone, who ironically studied marketing at Louisville, has always had a knack for finding a buck.

BUFFONE: After I got divorced from Linda (Doug's first wife), I was in tough shape. What really turned me around was meeting Dana.

Dana and I got fixed up by a friend of mine. When I met her, she didn't know a damn thing about my football career. So, the fact that she loved me for me made it special.

The twins—my baby girls Heather and Hailey.

People are funny because they think athletes have money to burn. When Dana and I decided to get married, there were actually people who said they thought she was marrying me for my money.

My money?

That's ridiculous.

Let me tell you about Dana.

She came from a little country town in South Carolina, but she won a national contest that instantly gave her "supermodel" assignments. Dana worked in New York, Germany, and France, as well as other big-time locations.

She was really in demand.

If anything, people should have been saying that I married her for her money.

I know at the time we met, she was making more money than I was. She was a legitimate six-figure model.

COPPOCK: Who falls for this handsome Italian guy.

BUFFONE: (Laughing) You know why Dana has been so good for me?

She doesn't back down. She's fiery. After my first marriage went up in flames, I ran wild for a few years. Dana really got me back on the straight and narrow.

I really wish Dana could have seen me play. I mean, she's seen me on tape, but I would have loved to have had her see me play in person. But I guess it really doesn't make any difference.

She loves me. That's what counts.

I felt the same way about our kids and my kids from the first marriage.

Listen, any football player always wants to show his kids just how tough the old man was. It probably goes back to me saying that all football players have what I called the "Neanderthal Gene."

I can tell Dana that one year, I took the field against Houston with a temperature of 104 degrees. I was just dead. I lasted eight plays before I collapsed. The doctors thought I had Legionnaires disease. I had pneumonia; I landed in Chicago and went straight to the hospital.

You know we lost that game to the Oilers by about 50 points (47–0). I remember on the plane ride back, our coach at the time, Jack Pardee, told me he was going to leave the club. I really wasn't that surprised.

Word in the locker-room was that Pardee had put his house up for sale. When I asked him why he wanted to leave, he told me bluntly, "Staying with the Bears is like pissing up a rope."

COPPOCK: Buffone is a devout Catholic. As we mentioned earlier, years ago, he actually gave thought to becoming a priest. If he had become a man of the cloth, Rush Street would have lost one heck of a player.

Doug was reluctant to kiss and tell with the girls he had dated in the years he spent back in the tiny town of Yatesboro, Pennsylvania.

Understandable for a class guy.

Tell the house about your fiery, youthful passion.

BUFFONE: Fiery back then meant a kiss lasting longer than 10 seconds. That was it.

COPPOCK: Did you get to first base?

BUFFONE: No, I tripped over the chalk.

COPPOCK: Ahhh, youth.

BUFFONE: Those were the days...

COPPOCK: I got the feeling as I looked at the gleam in his eye that he would trade just about anything to have a shot at being young again, if maybe for just one night, whether it be playing in a high school football game, hanging out with his teenage friends, or even enjoying that one fiery kiss.

Just one more time.

BUFFONE: I'm not afraid of dying. I'm not afraid to meet my maker; it's the other guy that scares me. I just know I'm gonna miss all this. I've had a great life and I want to keep living it. I believe in heaven, sure. But I like it here, too.

COPPOCK: I hear ya, pal. The memories, the Bears, the teammates, O.B., Dana, your kids, living each day as if it were your last, all make life worth living.

BUFFONE: Someday, it has to end for all of us. No regrets. God, I've been blessed with a great wife, wonderful kids, and memorable friends.

Acknowledgments

COPPOCK: The richness of your life, so many great moments, so many thrills and experiences the average person simply will never experience. What say you roll up the sleeves on the Cardinals' "billboard" and offer up some love to those people who have truly had profound effects on your life. I know we're bound to miss some people, but I also know those people already grasp how much you care about them.

BUFFONE: I want to begin with Frank Zuchelli, my high school football coach. He got me the "ride" at Louisville. If not for him, who the hell knows what I would have done with my adult life.

Dick Butkus: He's the greatest player in NFL history. He was also my roommate for years. I love "Paddles" like a brother.

Trainer Freddie Caito and strength coach Clyde Emerich: My guys. Without their skill and dedication, I just don't play 14 years in the NFL. I can't thank Freddie and Clyde enough. Caito kept my body from breaking while Clyde put me on a weight training program that carried me throughout my NFL career.

George Halas and the McCaskey family: Sure, the Old Man and I went to war a couple of times, but I truly believe the McCaskeys know just how much I loved the coach. The first time I shook hands with Halas, I shook hands with Herbert Hoover, Jim Thorpe, and street cars. I still miss Papa Bear.

My children, Ryan, Heather, Hailey, Doug Jr., Talleri, and Stephanie: You know what a blessing really is? It's when you think about your kids during their growing-up years and realize they've never really caused you a lick of trouble. They all have minds of their own and they will always have my unconditional love.

My brothers mean so damn much to me. *Sammy* walked away from a college scholarship because he believed in his heart that he should fight for our country during Vietnam. How many guys did that? *Joe* has become a highly successful businessman and genuine leader. *Dennis* is the classic outdoors man. He can spot a squirrel 500 yards away.

Let me tell you something; sure, I played football, but the fact is that these guys were all every bit as tough as I was, maybe even tougher. A guy never had a better support system.

My sisters, Tina, Donna Jean, and Debbie: I guess there were times I was a pain to be around them, but again, they were all about support. They are special, so special to me.

Norm Van Lier: God, he was tough, but his soul was enormous. He died much too young. I often dream about doing just one more radio show with Norm. You could feel his competitive drive. You could almost taste his football mentality.

Mitch Rosen, WSCR: Mitch is the rare program director who actually has a heart. He sees creativity beyond dollar signs. Mitch has made life very comfortable for O.B. and myself.

Ed O'Bradovich: Beneath those dark, brooding eyes, there is a smile that can light up a room.

Dan Bernstein, WSCR: Hey, buddy, I know you're hellfire and damnation on the air, but I also know you're one heck of a guy. Congratulations on a truly fine career.

Dan McNeil: Coppock, you probably know him better than I do. What I understand about Mac is that he's outrageous, flamboyant, and colorful.

Jim Memolo: We worked so well together. Jim tossed me the ball and I did my best to run with it. Jim, you never cared that I was the so-called "star." That's the mark of a pro.

Laurence Holmes, WSCR: A passionate workaholic. His career will eventually land him on one of the national TV networks.

Matt Spiegel, WSCR: He is just so damn versatile. A tremendous interviewer.

John Colletti: You are the heart and soul of Gibsons.

Ex-Bears Dan Hampton and Steve McMichael: With all due respect to Mike Singletary, Mike isn't in Canton without you guys up front. I just wish to hell I could have had 10 years with you guys on my side of the ball.

Kevin Yal, longtime business associate: Kevin passed far too young. He had so much imagination, so much drive. It seemed like every time he got involved in something new, he was always ahead of his time. He would have been a great marketing director for the NFL.

Sid Luckman, legendary Bears QB: Sid took the country boy from the mining country by the hand and gave him an education about Chicago's ins and outs. He was kind of like a second father.

Jerry Buffone: My cousin was a terrific athlete at Louisville. His top sport was baseball. He drew raves from Tommy Lasorda. I always admired the way Jerry carried himself. He's always been a stand-up guy.

Tony Bernardi: Tony was a major player during my growing-up years. He helped coach the football, basketball, and baseball teams when I was in high school. Tony was tough and demanding, but he also was fair. He really made you earn his approval. How tough was this guy? Think about Gene Hackman in Hoosiers. Tony once got so mad at our JV basketball team that he went ahead and played four guys rather than five just to make a point. All our guys wanted his approval.

Larry Wolfe: How can any one man have so much toughness while still having so much uncommon decency?

Sam LaRocco: He owns Fat Sam's in Orland Park. A real-life character. The only guy I know who was baptized at Sea World. No kidding.

Steve Lombardo: My Gobson's buddy, you're the best damn restaurant manager in this business.

I can't thank Jack McHugh enough. He's a prolific businessman who took a young Italian kid from Western Pennsylvania and taught him the ropes.

Chet Coppock: Okay, Coppock, you finally talked me into this book. You are the "Godfather of Sports Talk Radio" and one helluva writer.

Epilogue

Closure.

April 24, 2015. Overcast and rainy. Just six days after Doug's passing there was still an air of disbelief, a surrealistic feeling that something must be wrong.

But the Good Lord had put forth the call to his gridiron soldier from Western Pennsylvania. So it was that Doug was buried with a small private ceremony at Chicago's Graceland Cemetery on North Clark Street—just a 3-wood and a wedge up the street from Cubs Park. Poor Dana, Doug's widow, fought the brave fight to maintain a smile during the service, but her feelings melted in tears as we all paid our final respects.

Watching Dana lean over Doug's casket to offer a soft farewell was beyond poignant. You wept for Doug but you also wept for Dana and Doug's kids from his two marriages.

I felt lost. I still do. I lost a guy who was truly loyal, truly my friend as he had been to so many others. I couldn't help but reflect on comments made the night before by Dan Hampton, Eddie O'Bradovich, and Larry Wolfe, Doug's best and most trusted confidante. You'd have to know Larry up close and personal to know just why he would wave a poster-size cover of this book in front of the assembled congregation.

Larry wasn't hustling used cars or trying to use his time to present an infomercial. It was simply the Wolfe-man exhibiting his classically offbeat sense of humor. To know Larry is an education in giggles. The guy, like Doug, is an American original.

Following the burial, a modest crowd gathered at Dana's residence to share thoughts and a little booze.

I was fortunate enough to converse with Doug's cousin Jerry, who spoke with enormous pride about his cousin, the cousin who followed him to Louisville in a "package deal" 50-plus years ago.

Jerry said, "I always felt that Doug's greatest salesman was in fact Doug Buffone. Doug sold himself without really knowing it, whether he was playing football for Halas, running a restaurant, or talking on radio.

"If I lived a second life, I know what I would do to be successful. Just use the criteria that Doug put down for us. But that comes with one problem. I'm not Doug Buffone—nobody is. I doubt we'll see another guy like him—ever. There will never be another guy quite like Doug Buffone."

Jerry is a stand-up guy. He'll tell you he should have pursued his dream of playing major league baseball rather than "wasting four years at Louisville." Hell, the Boston Red Sox were just crazy about Jerry. The BoSox thought Jerry Buff might be another Frank Malzone.

As for me, seeing the people who surrounded Doug for so many years, I learned yet another lesson about my buddy.

Doug could never be a braggart, could never be an ego-driven louse. Why? His Western Pennsylvania roots, his mom and pop, his siblings, and extended family wouldn't stand for it.

To them, to all of you, I hope you always remember this about Doug Buffone.

He dripped with class.

He loved people and people loved him back in waves.

Buff could never showboat—he was just too big a man, a man to be admired. A simple man. Yet a man who achieved iconic status.

—Chet Coppock
April 29, 2015

In Memoriam

After Doug's passing on April 20, 2015, there was an outpouring of love for No. 55. It came in the form of articles, statements, tweets, sports radio callers, recounted stories, and raised glasses. Here are just a few, as we remember our good friend, Doug Buffone.

> "We are terribly saddened to hear of Doug's passing. He will always be celebrated as one of the Bears greats for his contributions to his team and the fans who loved him. There was no one tougher on Sundays than Doug Buffone. And he proved it each week over his 14-year career, a tenure record he shared with another great, Bill George, for 33 seasons. His retirement ended a link to our founder as he was the last active player to play for George Halas."
>
> —Bears Chairman George McCaskey

> "He was as big of a sweetheart as he was devastating as a linebacker."
>
> —*Chicago Tribune* columnist Steve Rosenbloom

> "He was a great player and a great friend. I have nothing but great memories about him.... Doug was a Bear. Besides being a hell of a football player, he was a hell of a guy."
>
> —Hall of Famer Mike Ditka

> "He wasn't worried about his awards or anything else. He just did the job. And that's what made him such a great guy, a great character, a great person."
>
> —Hall of Famer Dick Butkus

"We were all lucky to know Doug Buffone."

—CBSSports columnist Tim Baffoe

"I produced every WGN football broadcast, college and pro, for a quarter-century or more. I learned early on that the name Chicago Bears and the term 'linebacker' were synonymous. Almost from the time George Halas brought the Decatur Staleys to Chicago to become the Bears, great linebackers developed into legends. So it was that Doug Buffone, from 1966 to 1979, took his rightful place in this historical parade of stars. Doug Buffone fit the bill the way Halas literally drew it up. He was tough, smart, intense, and powerful. Those were the components the Papa Bear wanted and got. But Doug had still another attribute. He was well-spoken. This uncanny ability was to lead him to a fine analytical career in broadcasting after his playing days. Personally, I wouldn't have been surprised if former linebacker Doug Buffone had gone into politics. Doug always seemed to have it all."

—Legendary WGN Producer Jack Rosenberg

"He was Mr. Chicago Bear. Everything you would want out of a football player and a person, that was Doug Buffone."

—Ex-Bear Doug Plank

"RIP, Doug Buffone. A classic Bear.

—*Sports Illustrated* senior writer Peter King

"The most genuine man the business has ever introduced me to."

—670 The Score host Jason Goff

"Rest in peace, 55. The next game won't be the same without you."

—WGN Radio host Adam Hoge

"Being around Doug Buffone was like getting a Post Graduate Degree in Football and in life. He made time for everybody. Universally loved & respected. He was just the best and we all miss him terribly."

—120 Sports and 670 The Score host Laurence Holmes

"One time for Doug Buffone! It was an honor to share the #55 with the first legend to wear it."

—7-Time Pro Bowler Lance Briggs

"He gave me a big bear hug last time I saw him several months ago. A big hug from a big Bear. I never saw him play, but Doug is my favorite Bear."

—670 The Score host Chris Rongey

"Today is a sad day for Bears nation. We lost one of our greats. Doug Buffone will be missed. #dougbuffone. #bearslegend #55"

—2005 NFL Defensive Player of the Year Brian Urlacher

"Doug Buffone was a terrific person, he taught me tons about football and about life. I'll never forget the laughs. Rest in peace, my friend."

—ESPN's Mike Greenberg

"I was always a bit envious of my co-workers at The Score who had had the opportunity to work with Doug. I was also skeptical of the tales told about this man and the soft touch which countered a knockout punch. And then I had the chance to work with Doug. We watched a Bears game together and conducted the postgame show. He yelled, he screamed, he ate, he smiled, and he laughed. Afterward, he drove me back to the city from the suburbs, and we had a wonderful conversation. The soft side is real, and I'm lucky to have witnessed it."

—670 The Score/WBBM host Mark Grote

"Will always remember his generosity & kindness. Doug made the world a better place. He will be missed."

—ESPN Radio host Jeff Dickerson

"I loved watching Doug Buffone as a Bears fan, enjoyed his company even more as a friend and co worker. #RIPDoug"

—Fox 32 Sports anchor Lou Cannelis

"Cannot tell you how sad I am to hear of the passing of Doug Buffone. Doug was 'The Best'! My wife & I lost a great friend!"

—ESPN Radio host Fred Huebner

"When I think of Doug Buffone, I think of a great person, a great human being, a great father, and a great husband. I do not even think about the football player. Doug was a Chicago guy and a Score guy. There will never be another Doug Buffone."

—670 The Score operations director Mitch Rosen

"I'm not saying anything that every single other person hasn't already echoed when I say that Doug was a special man who led a special life—albeit one that was cut too short. It really hurt hearing the news Monday that Big Doug was gone. Truly shocking, but after the hurt subsided, the great memories started flooding in and a smile came to my face. And that's the feeling I want to remember going forward when I think of Doug Buffone."

—670 The Score reporter/host David Schuster

"The simplistic nature of how my dad handled life was really beautiful. For example as he drove along the road he would always stop to give money to poor people. He would just say that someday, 'That might be me out there, so I better help him because someday he may help me.' My dad always believed that we're all in this together. His passion for the Bears and the city of Chicago really was his way of reaching out to people. People he truly loved. I simply could not have been more fortunate to have him as my dad."

—Doug's son, Ryan Buffone

"Being with Doug the last 49 years, I know that no one person could love a family more than Doug. I know that no one person that played the game of football loved it more than Doug did. The bottom line is he was true and loyal to his family, to football, and to his friends. I cannot tell you how much I will miss him."

—Ex-Bear and 670 The Score Bears postgame host Ed O'Bradovich